Modern Peacemakers

Aung San Suu Kyi

Activist for Democracy in Myanmar

MODERN PEACEMAKERS

Modern Peacemakers

Aung San Suu Kyi

Activist for Democracy in Myanmar

Judy L. Hasday, Ed. M.

CHELSEA HOUSE
PUBLISHERS
An imprint of Infobase Publishing

Aung San Suu Kyi

Copyright © 2007 by Infobase Publishing

All rights reserved. No part of this book may be reproduced or utilized in any form or by any means, electronic or mechanical, including photocopying, recording, or by any information storage or retrieval systems, without permission in writing from the publisher. For information, contact:

Chelsea House
An imprint of Infobase Publishing
132 West 31st Street
New York, NY 10001

Library of Congress Cataloging-in-Publication Data
Hasday, Judy L., 1957-
　　Aung San Suu Kyi : activist for democracy in Myanmar / Judy L. Hasday.
　　　　p.　cm. — (Modern peacemakers)
　　Includes bibliographical references and index.
　　ISBN-13: 978-0-7910-9435-8 (hardcover)
　　ISBN-10: 0-7910-9435-9 (hardcover)
　　1. Aung San Suu Kyi. 2. Burma—Politics and government—1948– 3. Democracy—
Burma. 4. Women political activists—Burma—Biography. I. Title. II. Series.
　　DS530.68.A85H36 2007
　　959.105092—dc22
　　[B]　　　　　　　　　　　　　　　　　　　　　　　　　　　　　　2007002069

Chelsea House books are available at special discounts when purchased in bulk quantities for businesses, associations, institutions, or sales promotions. Please call our Special Sales Department in New York at (212) 967-8800 or (800) 322-8755.

You can find Chelsea House on the World Wide Web at
http://www.chelseahouse.com.

Text design by Annie O'Donnell
Cover design by Takeshi Takahashi

Printed in the United States of America

Bang FOF 10 9 8 7 6 5 4 3 2 1

This book is printed on acid-free paper.

All links and Web addresses were checked and verified to be correct at the time of publication. Because of the dynamic nature of the Web, some addresses and links may have changed since publication and may no longer be valid.

TABLE OF CONTENTS

CHAPTER 1

Life-changing Call

Aung San Suu Kyi, her husband, Michael Aris, and their sons, Alexander and Kim, had only been reunited for a few months before a late-evening phone call on March 31, 1988, separated the family again. At home in Oxford, England, Daw Suu (as Suu Kyi is known by friends) received a call from her native country, Burma. The call would set in motion events that no one, except maybe Daw Suu, could have foreseen. Ma Khin Kyi, Daw Suu's mother, had suffered a severe stroke and was in a Burmese hospital. There was no question that Daw Suu would fly home immediately. She did not want to pull Alexander and Kim out of school so late in the term, so Michael agreed to stay behind in England with the boys.

The trip home to Burma was not an easy one for Daw Suu. She is the daughter of a national hero, General Aung San, who was assassinated in 1947 while trying to form a transitional government in a newly independent Burma, so she fully understood sacrifice in the service of duty to country and devotion to freedom. In her absence, her homeland had been thrust into turmoil by a military

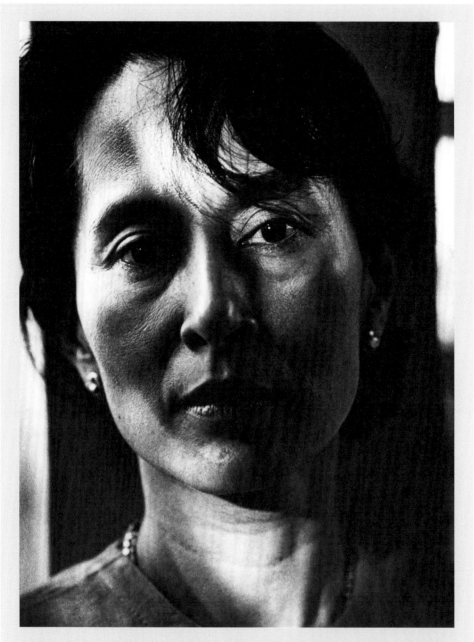

As the daughter of a national hero, Aung San Suu Kyi was guaranteed a place in Burmese history. When she returned to Burma in 1988 to care for her mother, she embarked upon a path that would make her a part of the country's history for her own work.

coup. The people of Burma, who had been living in a prosperous country, had come to live in one choked by corruption and abject poverty.

In 1962, Burmese General Ne Win led a military takeover of the country. Control was swift and total—all of Burma's banks, schools, infrastructure, and even businesses were seized by Ne Win's regime. He consolidated power, arresting members of the parliament and appointing military officers to government posts. Ne Win's new Burma Socialist Program Party (BSPP), a one-party state government, knew little about running day-to-day affairs, and it wasn't long before the country felt the impact of ineffective governance. Food and fuel shortages were widespread, but Burma was no longer a democracy, so its people had no voice in affairs of the government. Anyone who dared to speak out against the regime was imprisoned or killed. Unrest among the Burmese people grew as conditions worsened.

DRAWN IN

Two weeks before Ma Khin Kyi's stroke, a fight broke out between some students and some male locals at a teahouse in Rangoon. During the altercation, one student was stabbed. All the local men were arrested, but they were later released without being charged, after it was learned that one of the men was the son of an official in Ne Win's government. The release of the locals outraged students and civilians in cities and towns all over Burma. On March 13, protesters began to take their anger against the government into the streets, where they called for an end to the repressive regime.

Ne Win's response was violent and brutal. He ordered riot police and military soldiers to descend upon the protesters in the streets, which resulted in a fierce confrontation. As students and police clashed, hundreds of people were killed and countless others were beaten and thrown in jail. Battles between police and demonstrators continued throughout the month, ending in hundreds more deaths and arrests.

Daw Suu arrived in Rangoon in the midst of the government's crackdown on the civil unrest. Although she spent the next three months at her mother's bedside at Rangoon General Hospital, Daw Suu could look out the hospital room window and see clashes break out between protesters and police in the streets. What she could not see firsthand, Daw Suu heard about on the news. In one violent encounter between students and police on the Rangoon University campus on June 21, special antiriot units called Lon Htein fired tear gas and rifles into the crowd, killing 80 civilians. During the confrontation, 20 Lon Htein were also killed.

Daw Suu worried about the escalating violence. She believed that only peaceful dialogue with the government would bring about change. She wondered how long she could remain uninvolved in her beloved country's internal strife.

During this time of turmoil, it was also becoming clear that Daw Suu's mother was not showing any signs of improvement. When there was nothing more that could be done for her mother in the hospital, Daw Suu decided it was time to take Ma Khin back home, to her house on University Avenue. At least at home, Ma Khin would be in a familiar place, surrounded by the many friends she had made over the years. Among those who visited were U Tin Oo and U Nu, both of whom were intimately familiar with Ne Win's iron-fisted rule. U Tin Oo had been a soldier in the Burmese Army since the days of fighting for independence alongside Aung San. When Ne Win overthrew the government, U Tin Oo, who had earned the rank of general, was imprisoned. U Nu was prime minister of Burma when Ne Win seized power. The men spoke to Daw Suu about a movement under way in Burma, a movement toward a free and democratic country, much like the one her late father had envisioned 40 years earlier. They wanted Daw Suu to join them in the struggle.

8-8-88

It seemed for a brief moment that no democracy movement led by the people would be necessary. On July 23, without any prior warning, General Ne Win appeared on television to announce

---

Honorifics

The Burmese do not have a system of family names. Despite their deep feelings about family, the Burmese give each individual his own name, which is often different from the name of any other member of the family. To add to that individuality, a Burmese woman does not take her husband's name upon marriage. As is done in English, the Burmese language uses prefixes in front of one's proper name, such as *U, Daw, Maung,* and *Ma,* in much the same way as Mr. or Mrs. are used in English. Age, however, is an important part of determining which prefix to use. The word *U* means "uncle" and *Daw* means "aunt," so these words would not be used to address young children. *Maung* means "younger brother" and is appropriate for a boy, but when he gets older, the prefix changes to *Ko,* which means "older brother." For females of any age, however, *Ma* is the prefix used, which literally means "sister."

Burmese prefixes are also often determined by a person's standing. For example, a young man who has achieved a position of high standing would be addressed as U instead of Ko or Maung. Conversely, if an older man is of lower status, instead of being addressed as U, he may still be addressed as Ko or Maung. Daw is used for Burmese women of high standing. It would be proper to address Khin Kyi, who was an ambassador of Burma and considered a woman of great stature, as Daw Khin Kyi. In the case of Aung San's family, when the children were named, each son had his father's name in addition to his own (Aung San U and Aung San Lin), and Suu Kyi was given her father's name (Aung San), her grandmother's name (Suu), and her mother's name (Kyi).

that he would resign his position as chairman of the BSPP. Ne Win seemed to take responsibility for the current state of affairs in the country, when he suggested that the country hold a referendum to determine whether the people wanted a multiparty system of government. Not to be seen as intimidated or marginalized in any way by his decision to step down, Ne Win also warned the demonstrators that to continue to do so would have grave consequences. "When the military shoot, they shoot to hit. They won't shoot into the air to frighten."[1]

Although the BSPP cabinet appeared to accept Ne Win's resignation, it was later viewed as a ploy to step out of the spotlight and control things from behind the scenes. Feelings of joy were quickly overruled by the news that the BSPP central committee rejected the call for a referendum and instead elected Sein Lwin, who was known among the civilian population as "the butcher." The appointment of Lwin as chairman of the State Council evoked even more outrage and anger in the streets of Burma. Protesters redoubled their efforts to demonstrate opposition to the regime. Students were no longer the lone participants in the uprising. They were joined en masse by many others who were fed up with the state of the country, including businessmen, farmers, dock workers, lawyers, and Buddhist monks.

Demonstration organizers wanted to stage a huge strike to show unified strength to the government. They chose August 8, 1988, to hold the strike, believing that the repetition of the number eight would bring them luck. Hundreds of thousands of workers walked off their jobs and went out to the street to join in protest, eventually gathering in front of City Hall. Throughout the day there were speeches given against the government policies all Burmese people endured. As Daw Suu said later of the demonstration, "They wanted no more of the authoritarian rule . . . that had impoverished Burma intellectually, politically, morally, and economically."[2]

The protest strike was a peaceful one, until night fell. Then, just before midnight, truckloads of heavily-armed soldiers pulled up to the crowd, got out, and surrounded the workers. Frightened

After the military takeover of the Burmese government in 1962, there were numerous demonstrations against what became an oppressive regime. Above, marchers from all strata of society in Rangoon demonstrate against 26 years of authoritarian rule on September 1, 1988.

but unbending in their resolve, the crowd broke out in song. To everyone's horror, the soldiers responded by opening fire on the unarmed demonstrators. One witness described the scene:

> Soldiers pointed their automatic rifles in the crowds. Then, suddenly, the two warning pistol shots came and within seconds the automatic rifle shots took the center stage and scores of people, young and old, fell to their death instantly. The streets near the City Hall turned chaotic with people screaming, running and taking cover in random directions. More truckloads of soldiers were sent to Shwegondine Road where whole columns of demonstrators were gunned down. The casualties were estimated over 2,000. The shooting continued until 3:00 A.M the next day. No one knew how many demonstrators were killed in total.[3]

After the massacre, which became known as the Four Eights strike, U Tin Oo and U Nu again approached Daw Suu. Daw Suu knew she could no longer remain quietly on the sidelines. The time had come for her to help her country. As Daw Suu later said, "I could not as my father's daughter remain indifferent."[4] She agreed to get involved in a movement to bring democracy to Burma. By doing so, she put herself on a collision course with the very regime that had exhibited no respect for the value of the lives of those who voiced opposition. The phone call brought her back to Burma for her mother. The state of her country was now bringing her into a political unrest that could cost Daw Suu her very freedom.

CHAPTER 2

Land of the Pagodas

T he country of Aung San Suu Kyi's ancestors has a diverse population, one that has played a major role in defining its past, its politics, its culture, and its present. It has been described as "a country where magnificent and ancient Buddhist temples gaze out serenely over a nation restless for change. Myanmar has plenty of wonders for the eye—sinuous, life-giving rivers, lush mountain forests, and intricately drawn cities—but it can also trouble the soul."[5] Once, Myanmar was a Southeast Asian state struggling for its independence from British colonial rule. Today, however, the country has yet to realize the freedom and democracy the majority of its people have struggled and died for since a dictatorship seized control after the military coup of 1962.

A country slightly smaller than the state of Texas, Myanmar is part of the region in the world known as Southeast Asia. It is situated among several neighboring countries, including Bangladesh and India to its northwest, China to its north and east, and Laos and Thailand to its southeast. One-third of Myanmar's border forms an

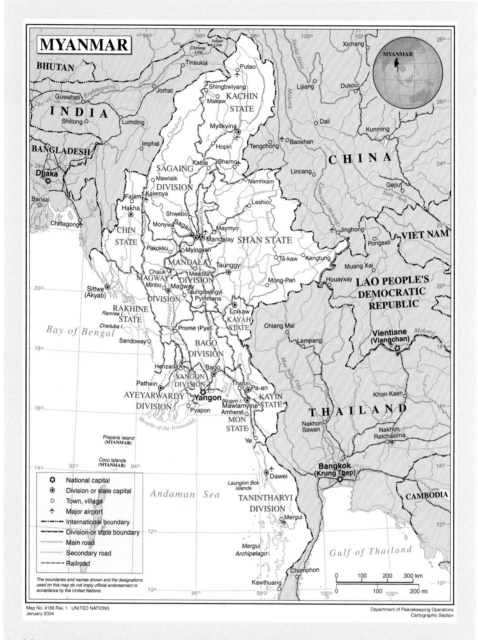

Myanmar, formerly known as Burma, is a small country in Southeast Asia. The national capital, Yangon (formerly Rangoon), is located in the south, near the coast.

uninterrupted coastline where the Bay of Bengal lies to its south-west and the Andaman Sea lies to its south. A country of diverse terrain, Myanmar is lush and rugged, with an architectural land-scape that reflects its rich history and cultural development.

The southern region of Myanmar comprises mostly the vast western slopes of the Bilauktaung Range, which forms the northern base of the Malay Peninsula. The northern part of Myanmar consists largely of the expansive river valley of the Irrawaddy. The Irrawaddy, Myanmar's longest river, starts its descent high up in the eastern edge of the Himalaya Mountains, flowing down through vast mountainous ravines in the northern part of the country. As it travels southward to the Bay of Bengal, the Irrawaddy widens out into one of the largest river deltas in Asia. The majority of Myanmar's population lives in the lowlands region of the river valley, where the fertile delta soil makes the area one of the great rice-growing regions in the world.

A COUNTRY RICH IN RESOURCES

Because of the two key components, rich soil and moderate-to-tropical climate, Myanmar is rich in natural resources. About 60 percent of the population works in the agricultural and forestry industries. Rice crops account for almost half of Myanmar's agricultural production, making it one of the country's most important economic resources. Other crops include corn, pea-nuts, beans, oilseeds, and sugarcane. Tropical fruits such as cit-rus, bananas, mangoes, and guavas grow in the coastal regions. Myanmar's forests cover almost 50 percent of the country and contain more than 250 commercially serviceable kinds of timber and oil-bearing trees, including rubber, cinchona, acacia, bam-boo, ironwood, mangrove, coconut, betel palm, oak, and pine. Myanmar's most valuable forest wood is teak, which is primarily used in making furniture. The majority of the world's remaining supply of teak is found in Myanmar, making it a valuable resource for the country's economy.

The seas off Myanmar's southern coast and its two primary rivers, the Irrawaddy and the Sittang, are home to a variety of fish, and the fishing industry is the third largest contributor to the country's gross domestic product. Myanmar has almost 300 species of freshwater fish (called *nga*), like the little-known *mrigal*. Other, more commonly known marine fish include varieties of mackerel, mullet, sea perch, grouper, snapper, halibut, and flounder. Freshwater fish include tilapia, catfish, anchovy, and carp. Shrimp alone accounts for about 50 percent of Myanmar's fishery export. Along with other fish, shrimp and prawns are exported to countries such as Canada, Australia, China, and several European countries.

Myanmar's mountainous areas in the west and along the Tenasserim coast hold a wealth of minerals. Several natural deposits of precious stones, including jade, rubies, and sapphires, are found in the village of Mogok, a centuries-old center of the Myanmarese ruby trade. The Baldwin Mines in the Shan State, northwest of Lashio, are sources of copper, nickel, silver, lead, and zinc. Some petroleum has been found east of the Irrawaddy River, and extensive natural gas resources have been found in the Bay of Bengal. Pearls are harvested from the *Pinctada maxima* oysters in the waters off the Myeik Archipelago, a chain of about 800 islands off the southern coast. Myanmar is also a major producer of illegal opium. Heroin is produced in labs in a region known as the Golden Triangle in the northern area of the country, bordering Laos and Thailand, and contributes to a lucrative and large black-market trade in the drug.

EARLY INHABITANTS

The people of Myanmar belong to a variety of racial and ethnic groups, many of whom have at one time or another historically dominated a certain region of the country. Today, Myanmar's people are the Mon, Burmans, Kachins, Chins, Shans, Rakhine, and Karen. Each of these groups has controlled a particular part

This photo shows peasants with oxcarts crossing the Moei river from Thailand into Myanmar. Myanmar is a lush country with access to many bodies of water, making agriculture and fishing two of its primary industries.

of the country at some point in Myanmar's history. Although Burmese is the major and official language, there are more than 100 local and regional dialects of the language spoken throughout the country.

Artifacts found in Myanmar indicate that the Mon were probably the earliest people to migrate down from central Asian countries, which include Tibet and China, and settle in the Irrawaddy Valley around 3000 B.C. Believed to be a people of Malayo-Indonesian lineage, the Mon are related to the early inhabitants of the neighboring Southeast Asian countries of Thailand and Cambodia, who also spoke Mon-Khmer languages. The Mon established a significant capital in Burma at

Thaton, an important location for trade near the waters of the Andaman Sea, and engaged in trade with India's King Asoka. The Mon called the lower delta region *Suvannabhumi* ("the land of gold") and later converted to Theravada Buddhism, a conservative branch of Buddhism based on the Four Noble Truths: Life means suffering; the origin of suffering is attachment; the cessation of suffering is attainable; and there is a path to the cessation of suffering.

Siddhartha Gautama

Buddha, as he is known in the Western world as well as in Asia, was born Siddhartha Gautama in Lumbini, Nepal, in the sixth century B.C. Siddhartha was born of privilege; his father, Suddhodana, was the ruler of the Sakya people, and he expected his son to one day be a ruler, too.

Siddhartha married at age 16, according to custom; he and his wife, Yasodhara, had a son, Rahula. As a prince, Siddhartha spent many years in seclusion, as his father had ordered. Although Suddhodana gave Siddhartha many extravagances, the young man was discontent. He ventured out of seclusion and, struck by the suffering of his people, he gave up his princely world and set out to find a method to overcome life's trials.

Initially, Siddhartha focused on meditating with religious teachers. He lived a life of great deprivation. Later, however, after accepting food from a young girl, he denounced this path. He determined instead to follow a life of balance, which he called the Middle Way, and would advocate this life for others as well. At age 35, after his experience with the young girl, he meditated under the Bodhi tree and reached enlightenment. He announced that he had become completely awakened, had come to understand that ignorance is what causes suffering, and determined how to be rid of it. For the rest of his life, he taught others the path toward awakening and how to see reality as it truly is.

The origin of Buddhism can be traced back to the birth of Siddhartha Gautama in Nepal, around 563 B.C. The son of a wealthy landowner, Siddhartha spent his youth living a privileged life but grew unhappy when he was confronted with the realities that existed beyond his sheltered life, including aging, sickness, and death. Siddhartha gave up his privileged life to find enlightenment. While teaching the ways to avoid suffering, he became known as Buddha, which means "one who is awake." One writer described Buddhism in this way:

> Buddhism is a path of practice and spiritual development leading to Insight into the true nature of life. Buddhist practices such as meditation are means of changing oneself in order to develop the qualities of awareness, kindness, and wisdom. The experience developed within the Buddhist tradition over thousands of years has created an incomparable resource for all those who wish to follow a path—a path which ultimately culminates in Enlightenment or Buddhahood.[6]

The practice of Buddhism would become an integral part of the way Burma's people approached all aspects of life, and it would be passed down and taught to succeeding generations.

A KINGDOM IS BORN

The Mon were not alone in Burma for long. Another group known as the Pyu arrived from Tibet and settled inland from the Irrawaddy River in the northern region of Myanmar between the first century B.C. and A.D. 800. Both cultures flourished until the Burmans arrived in the ninth century and began controlling the settlement from the city of Pagan. Pagan became the capital of the first Burmese kingdom between A.D. 1044 and 1077, under King Anawrahta, the first great Burmese ruler. Anawrahta conquered both the Pyu and the Mon peoples and formed a united Burma.

There is evidence that Buddhism was practiced by the Mon and Pyu cultures long before King Anawrahta's reign:

> According to Mahavamsa, the Great Chronicle of Sri Lanka, the Emperor Asoka of India sent missionaries to nine countries in the 3rd Century B.C. It is said that the Venerable Sona and the Venerable Uttara were sent to propagate and teach Buddhism in Suvanabhumi (the "Golden Land")—present day Lower Myanmar and Thailand. According to Myanmar tradition it was two merchants from Okkala (modern Yangon) who had the privilege of offering the Buddha his first meal following his enlightenment.[7]

King Anawrahta made Theravada Buddhism the state religion of Pagan, after he successfully obtained Buddhist texts from the Mon state of Thaton. Under the spiritual guidance of Shin Arahan, a distinguished Mon monk from Thaton, Theravada Buddhism spread, from the borders of India in the west to part of Thailand, to the country's south.

Later migrations brought the Kachins, Chins, Shans, Rakhine, and Karen into Burma, but it was King Anawrahta who first unified the country. During his reign, the Golden Age of the city of Pagan ("Bagan" is now the official transliteration) begins the great era of pagoda building. A pagoda is

> a cone-shaped monumental structure built in memory of Buddha. . . . The finial, or decorative crowning ornament of the stupa, became more elongated and cylindrical until the stupa's upper portion took on an attenuated, tower-like appearance. This stupa form was adopted by Buddhism as an appropriate form for a monument enshrining sacred relics and became known to Westerners as a pagoda. The Buddhist pagoda was elaborated in Tibet into a bottle-shaped form.[8]

Over the next two centuries, some 13,000 temples, pagodas, and other religious buildings rose up against the city skyline.

Among the most striking features of Burmese architecture is the pagoda,
a cone-shaped monumental structure for enshrining sacred relics.
Above, three Buddhist monks walk around the massive Shwedagon
Pagoda in Yangon.

Of the thousands of pagodas and temples in Bagan constructed during King Anawrahta's reign, the very first was Shwesandaw Pagoda, a graceful, circular pagoda built at the center of his kingdom. Shwesandaw Pagoda is believed to enshrine a Buddha hair relic brought back from the Mon city of Thaton.

A COUNTRY GROWS

In the thirteenth century, Mongols led by Kublai Khan invaded Burma. The Mongols, a group of Asiatic people from what is now Mongolia, China, and Russia, were nomadic horsemen and superb warriors, who at one time established the largest land empire the world has ever seen. The Mongol invasion destroyed the unified kingdom of King Anawrahta. The Mon and the Burmans retreated to the south and founded the city of Bago. In the northern part of the country, the Shans established a kingdom at Innwa. Soon afterward, the Mon and the Shans were at war. It was

Rangoon's Pagodas

Although pagodas have primarily religious purposes, they have also been used as watchtowers, as vantage points for enjoying the view of the surrounding areas, and as guides for ships and other vehicles. Indeed, Shwedagon Pagoda in Yangon is one that can be seen for miles, not only because it rises nearly 328 feet (100 meters) into the sky, but also because of its sparkling golden dome. Shwedagon Pagoda is believed to have been constructed about 2,500 years ago. Legend has it that the structure contains eight strands of Buddha's hair, supposedly given to two brothers by the Buddha himself. Relics of earlier Buddhas reside here, as well.

Another golden pagoda is the Sule Pagoda, located in the center of downtown Yangon. While at 151 feet, it is notably during this period, in the 1600s and early 1700s, that the Europeans, including the British, Dutch, and French, started traveling into Asia and setting up trade along the Burmese coast. Thus began the influx of a European presence in the region, which exists to the present day.

The reunification of Burma resumed in the sixteenth century under the Toungoo Dynasty and lasted into the mid 1700s, before the Mon resumed control over Burma. The last Burmese dynasty occurred in 1752 under the rule of King Alaungpaya, who successfully fought off attempted invasions by the Chinese, the British, and the French, as they attempted to gain control of the country.

The British did not give up their quest to conquer Burma, however. When King Alaungpaya ventured too close to the Bengal border and conquered Rahkine in 1819, the British retaliated, and thus began the first Anglo–Burmese War. The British Raj in India sent invading armies in to conquer Rahkine. Then,

smaller than the Shwedagon, its octagonal shape makes it unusual. It is said to hold one hair of the Buddha and is more than 2,000 years old.

The Botahtaung Pagoda (*Botahtaung* translates as "leader" and "a thousand") is a sign of the importance of relics. It was given this name because more than 2,000 years ago, 1,000 military leaders traveled from India with relics of the Buddha, many of which are now on display in glass cases inside the pagoda. This pagoda also has a golden spire, measuring 131 feet, nearly as tall as the Sule Pagoda.

The Chauk Htat Gyi Pagoda is another pagoda that is special because of what lies inside. Specifically, it holds a reclining Buddha image that is one of the largest images in Myanmar. This building, built in 1907 and then rebuilt in 1966 because of damage from the elements, is notably newer than the others mentioned here.

British forces pushed farther and captured Tanintharyi, Assam, and Manipur. They extended their control to lower Burma in the mid-1800s, and by 1886, the British had successfully annexed the entire nation of Burma, making it a province of India, ruled through the Raj.

British occupation marked a time of unrest among the Burmese. In the early 1900s, the British decided to appease the Burmese by granting Burma some degree of autonomy. Many were still not satisfied, and in 1930 a Burmese rebel named Saya San led an armed revolt against his colonizers. The British crushed the rebellion, and San was executed.

In an effort to further appease Burma's discontented citizens, the British made the country a crown colony. It was too little, too late, for many—especially outspoken student activists who called for the British to leave and grant Burma's independence. One such activist was a Rangoon University Students' Union editor named Aung San. No one could imagine at the time of his appointment to the magazine in 1935 that Aung San would one day lead Burma to its independence. Nor could Aung San have known at that time that one day in the future, his own daughter would take up the cause of his beloved country.

CHAPTER 3

General's Dream

By the beginning of the twentieth century, Britain had successfully
completed its colonization of Burma. Colonization meant that
control over Burma's resources, economy, and government
rested with the British, which left very little say over the country's
status to the Burmese people. British rule had some advantages,
however. These included improvements in the country's infrastructure: Roads were paved, a railway was constructed through the
entire Irrawaddy Valley, and steamboats chugged along the length
of the river. Merchants exported Burma's natural and agricultural
resources, such as rubies, oil, timber, and rice. Burma's economic
health grew from British control, but it was the colonists, and not the
Burmese people, who most benefited from the prosperity.

Although the British maintained control of the colony of Burma,
they recognized that, in order to preserve some form of unity within
the country, they needed to allow the native inhabitants to be self-
sufficient. One way the British tried to do so was by encouraging the
various ethic groups, which included the Karen, Shans, Kachins, and

Chins, to participate in some form of self-governance. At the same time, however, British rule smothered much of Burmese culture beneath its own European ways. This was especially evident in the huge social disintegration that the British caused by demanding a clear separation of church and state. The British practiced Christianity, whereas most of Burma practiced the Buddhist faith. The British were unwilling to support Burmese Buddhism the way the monarchies had in the past.

Because of their experience in India, which had led to the revolt of 1857 to 1859, the British did not wish to touch the issue of religion and thus were unwilling to patronize Burmese Buddhism as the monarchy had done. Under the monarchy, church and state had shared a symbiotic relationship. Royal patronage of Burmese Buddhism had included both financial and moral support, and this had extended legitimacy and authority to the church. The British refusal to heed a plea by the clergy and church elders to continue the traditional church-state relationship resulted in the decline of the *sangha* and its ability to instill discipline in the clergy. (The sangha was the Buddhist monastic order, usually composed of monks, nuns, and laypeople.) This, in turn, lowered the prestige of the clergy and contributed to the rise of secular education and of a new class of teachers, depriving the sangha of one of its primary roles.[9] The sangha was a part, in concert with the Buddha and the *dharma* (teaching), of the Threefold Refuge, a basic creed of Buddhism.

SEEDS OF RESISTANCE TAKE ROOT

Because the sangha was weakened in its importance in Burmese society, its role as primary educator was diminished, as well. This contributed to the rise of secular education in the schools and new teachers in the classrooms, ones who taught both English and Burmese languages. Foreign Christian missionaries were encouraged to found schools and were even offered financial assistance as an incentive to do so. The missionaries worked as teachers, and their lessons promoted Christianity and criticized Buddhism and its way of life. All of the Burmese people did not just simply assimilate to the new culture, though, despite the lack of understanding about the Burmese culture and its people by the British and those in India charged with their governance. A group of young Burmese men in 1906 established the Young Men's Buddhist Association (YMBA) to bridge the gap between centuries of Burmese culture and traditions and the modernization brought on by British colonization.

Over time, the members of the YMBA took on some of the critical issues important to Burma's traditional and religious survival. They fought against the British policy of segregated railcar compartments for Europeans only and the sell-off of Burmese land to foreign investors and developers. In addition, they were vehemently vocal in their opposition to what became known as the "shoe question." The British, in another example of insensitivity to Buddhist traditions, proclaimed that visitors to temples, shrines, and pagodas did not have to remove their shoes before entering any of these sacred places, as had been the custom. The shoe question became the focus of the YMBA's struggle in resistance to the British imperial rule over Burma. It

> symbolized this struggle in such a simple and elemental way and since close links between the Buddhist values and Buddhism were under threat, it became the perfect point of departure from diverse ethnic and other considerations to become a national movement for freedom, not as pleaders but as antagonists to the British rule to gain national independence.[10]

Many Burmese were motivated to maintain a strong cultural and religious identity. Another driving force that fueled the unrest and resistance to colonial rule rose from the British refusal to share the country's growth and prosperity with the Burmese. Like the citizens of other countries, such as the colonists in America who rose up and rebelled against British rule in 1776, Burma's people wanted their independence and the right to self-govern. Slowly, their resistance gained traction.

The British Colonial Empire

The British Empire reached the peak of its power and influence around the late 1890s and early 1900s. It became the largest recognized imperial sovereignty that the modern world had ever seen. Adept at colonization, England spread its authority all over the world, influencing many other cultures in significant ways. There were many factors that made the growth of the empire advantageous. In the sixteenth century, for example, England was a poor country, and commercial gain was necessary. The acquisition of territories provided sources of raw materials and markets in which to trade goods.

Burma was just one of the many countries and lands to fall under the control of the British flag. One of the earliest successful British colonies was Jamestown, Virginia, which was established in North America in 1607. Over the next 200 years or more, England expanded its influence around the globe. In addition to controlling colonies in what would later become the United States, it asserted itself in other parts of North America, as well as in Central America and the Caribbean, South America, Europe and islands near it, Africa, the Antarctic region, Asia, Australia and the Pacific Islands, islands in the Atlantic, and islands in the Indian Ocean. The countries included Australia, Hong Kong, Ireland, New Zealand, South Africa, Rhodesia, Ghana, and Nigeria.

By 1921, the British Empire had power over almost one-quarter of the world's population and almost one-quarter of the total land on Earth. Although many areas became decolonized beginning in the 1960s, many still retained some relationship with their previous rulers. The British influence remains strong to this day; some former colonies follow the British legal system or the parliamentary system of government. Some use money units derived from the British pound sterling. Of course, the English language also continues to dominate in most former British colonies.

In 1920, the British announced the passage of the Rangoon University Act, which in effect limited higher educational opportunities to those of privilege.

> Only boarding students would be allowed to study in the university while day students were disqualified. This would enable only the rich to receive higher learning. Though a person matriculated, one had to pass a university entrance examination first before he/she could receive a university education.[11]

The act prompted Burma's university students to stage a strike in protest. Many people point to this protest as the beginning of Burma's move toward independence. As a result of the strike, provisions of the act were amended in a way that was acceptable to the students. The success of the protest showed many people in Burma that they could achieve change through peaceful and united resistance to unfair imperialist (British) actions. The actions of the students and those who protested with them led to the establishment of National Day, the day of all days to be celebrated in Burma as a symbol of the first step toward independence.

HERO FROM NATMAUK

While the beginning of a movement toward Burma's independence was taking shape, the future leader of that movement was just a five-year-old boy living in central Burma. Born on February 13, 1915, in Natmauk, Aung San was the youngest of six children of U Phar and Daw Suu. Aung San was the heir in an affluent rural family. His father was a lawyer, and the family was known for its prominent line of patriotic ancestors, which could be traced back to the British annexation of Burma in 1886.

Throughout much of his life, Aung San was described by those who knew him—from family and friends to teachers and political colleagues—as intelligent, aggressive, reticent, quick-tempered, and totally committed to seeing Burma gain its independence. An independent Burma was so much a part of Aung San's dreams, that even from a very young age he created stories where he had magical powers that he used to free Burma from the colonial rule of the British.

As Aung San matured, his commitment to seeing a free and sovereign Burma never wavered. He was also a voracious reader and extremely interested in politics, language, and religion. A former colleague, Professor Khynt Maung, described Aung San as "an intellectual by instinct." He went on to say that Aung San could also be totally undisciplined. "I knew him well and I knew people who were quite involved in his activities, and most said of him that he was extremely rude and very unpredictable. But, of course, he was a genius so people accepted his idiosyncrasies."[12] Aung San studied first in the Vernacular High School in Nat-mauk, and then in National High School in Yenangyaung. The National Schools in Burma had been established in response to the 1920 Rangoon University Act. According to Aung San Suu Kyi, her father's desire to see Burma free of British control intensified while he was attending the National High School in Yenangyaung. Many of those who attended the National Schools were already budding, politically conscious intellectuals, and several would soon play a significant role in Burma's liberation from Britain, including civil rights revolutionary Nai Shwe Kyin; Burma's first prime minister, U Nu; and future dictator Ne Win.

The first serious challenge to British rule was unfolding while Aung San was still a National School student. Late in the year in 1930, Burmese peasants and farmers, discontented with sagging economic conditions, declining rice prices, and competition with Indian immigrants for the few jobs available, initiated a strike against the occupying British forces. They were led by Saya San, a Buddhist monk, physician, and astrologer, who named himself king and put together an army of rebels armed merely with spears and swords.

The rebellion lasted less than two years, and although the rebels could not match the military power and weaponry of the British and Indian forces, more than 3,000 casualties resulted.

Saya San, who was captured in 1931, was prosecuted in front of a special tribunal. Sentenced to death, Saya San was hanged at Tharrawaddy Jail. His leadership, however, proved an inspiration to the Burmese people, who wanted the British to leave Burma, and from him they learned how to organize resistance groups to challenge British control.

Aung San entered Rangoon University in 1932, the same year the Saya San Rebellion was crushed. Because the rebellion ultimately failed, he quickly recognized that the use of military force was probably going to be the only way for Burma to earn independence. Aung San was an exceptionally bright student, but his political interests and involvement as a student leader took most of his time. In 1935, U Nu was elected president of the Rangoon University Students' Union, and Aung San was elected secretary.

During his time at the university, Aung San also worked as an editor on the Students' Union magazine, as well as on the *Nagani,* or "Red Dragon," Book Club. In 1936, after U Nu published an article calling for the firing of a Burmese faculty member as a result of "alleged moral improprieties," British officials expelled both U Nu and Aung San from the university. The expulsions led to countrywide strikes by students, which quickly grew in size and scope. To quell the strikes, the British retracted the expulsions and permitted U Nu and Aung San to return to classes.

Despite losing a year of academic study, Aung San did not lose step with the cause for Burma's independence. When he returned to school, he was elected

President of the Rangoon University Students' Union, and [served] as one of the founders and President of All-Burma Students' Union. He also served, even as a student, along with another student representative, on the University Act Amendment Committee appointed by Government of the day early in 1938 and succeeded in getting a fairly progressive University Act passed by the Burma Legislature, and Act which had been the source of so much country-wide students' agitations and strikes in 1920 and 1936.[13]

In 1938, Aung San took another step in dedicating his time in the service of the political cause for freedom, when he joined the *Dobama Asiayone*, or "We Burmans Organization." Established in 1931 in support of the Saya San Rebellion, the members addressed each other as *Thakin*, a term that meant "Master" and was normally reserved as an expression of respect when addressing the British.

> As a Thakin leader, he was arrested and detained early in 1939 for being one of those leading "a conspiracy to overthrow Government by force" according to Government communiques of the day but was released shortly after. As General Secretary of the Thakin Party, "there was no doubt that he worked hard . . ." and was one of the triumvirate who made *Dohbama Asiayone* "such a subversive movement it today is," as written in Government records of that time, responsible for formulation of a number of important decisions and policies of the party.[14]

WAR AND LOVE

By 1940, Aung San, together with another Thakin, Kodaw Hmaing, had formed a political party they called the *Bama-htwet-yat Ghine*, or "Freedom Bloc," whose primary goal was to gain full independence for Burma. Aung San's political activities gained the attention of the British, who issued a warrant for his arrest. He went underground but continued his quest to free Burma from British control by seeking foreign support.

With the outbreak of World War II, a political rival, U Saw, became the third prime minister of Burma. Saw brokered a deal with the British (one later qualified as not applying to Burma by British Prime Minister Winston Churchill) to permit Burma full self-governing or dominion status at the end of the war. He also approached the Japanese, in the event that they invaded Burma. (Japan, Germany, and Italy were aligned as Axis powers, and Britain, the United States, and several other European countries were aligned as the Allied powers.) When the British learned of

U Saw's communication with the Japanese, he was arrested and sent to prison in Uganda for four years.

The Japanese, however, through one of Aung San's colleagues, agreed to train a group of Burmese Nationalists to fight the British while at the same time assisting Japan in its eventual invasion of Burma. Aung San, along with 29 others, including Thakin Shu Maung (later known as Ne Win), Bo Ye Htut, Bo Kyaw Zaw, Ba Maw, and Bo Hmu Aung, were smuggled out of Burma and provided with military training and weapons. The group became known as the Thirty Comrades and formed the core of the Burmese Independence Army (BIA). Aung San was made a commander, and in 1942, the BIA marched into Burma with their Japanese allies and drove the British from Burma. Ba Maw was named Prime Minister, Thakin Nu was the Minister of Foreign Affairs, and Aung San was appointed Minister of Defense and Commander of the BIA.

Although successful in driving the British from their homeland, several BIA soldiers, including Aung San, contracted malaria, an often fatal disease transmitted through the bite of an infected mosquito. The 27-year-old General Aung San was taken to Rangoon General Hospital, where he was given a hero's care by one of the hospital's best caregivers, senior nurse Khin Kyi. Aung San had a reputation for being moody and difficult; Khin Kyi was known for her patience, kindness, and inner strength. Aung San came to respect her, and the two soon developed a mutual affection. Not long after, they fell in love; they were married on September 6, 1942.

The newlyweds settled in a comfortable home in Rangoon, the capital of free Burma. Khin Kyi had married a man who, for most of his life, had dreamed of an independent Burma. Aung San was a loving husband and later a devoted father, but his love and loyalty to country was just as much a part of him as his wife and family. Khin Kyi had married not only an important Burmese military man, but also a national hero, much of whose impact on his beloved country was yet to come.

CHAPTER 4

Martyr's Daughter

General Aung San, although pleased that Burma was now free from British rule, had begun to have serious reservations about Japan's intentions. In the spring of 1943, Aung San visited Tokyo, where he was decorated by Emperor Hirohito for his military service. While he was there, a Japanese military colleague told him that the leaders in Tokyo were not really interested in aiding Burma's people in their fight to break free of British rule—they were more interested in Burma's natural resources, including its oil. Despite Prime Minister Tojo Hideki's assurances that Burma would be granted its independence at the end of 1943, it seemed that Japan viewed Burma not as a partner, but rather as a source of economic and military importance in its overall imperialistic strategies.

If the Burmese people thought that life under British rule was objectionable, they learned all too quickly that it could be even worse with their ambitious new allies. In reality, life under the Japanese military was harsh and at times even brutal:

The lives of Burmese people under Japanese occupation can be described as very grave and grim. Rich natural resources and food were exploited to feed Japanese soldiers in the front lines. This led to food scarcity and people died of preventable diseases for lack of medicine and basic necessities. Moreover, forced labour to construct the death railway which linked Thai and Burma killed as many as a hundred thousand of lives.[15]

Aung San realized that he had made a mistake in seeking the help of the Japanese. Secretly, Aung San began to organize the BIA and the Burmese populace to rise up against the Japanese. He realized that he would need the help and cooperation of the various political factions within his country, including the Karen National Organization and former associates from Dobama Asiayone, as well as Burmese socialists and communists.

To assist with unity, Aung San created a new party called the Anti-Fascist Organization (AFO; later expanded to the Anti-Fascist People's Freedom League, or AFPFL). Once he secured the cooperation of the diverse groups in Burma, most of whom had their own agendas, Aung San made contact with the British. The war had not been going well for the Japanese by this time, and Aung San approached a British government whose military was poised to reenter and take back Burma. Although the British agreed to Aung San's help in fighting the Japanese, many believed that the general recognized that the tide in the war had changed and he therefore wanted to seize the opportunity to switch to the winning side.

In March 1945, in conjunction with the Allied forces' advance into Burma, Aung San led his army into battle against the Japanese. By May, most of Burma, including the capital city of Rangoon, had been retaken by the Allies. For their cooperation, the BIA was given official recognition as part of the British Allied Forces. During victory celebrations held the following month, the AFO's red flag with its single white star flew next to Great Britain's Union Jack. Aung San had much to celebrate. His military had served the Allies well and had driven the Japanese out of Burma.

In 1942, Burmese Nationalists, in cooperation with the Japanese, drove the British out of Burma. When it became clear that the Japanese had imperialistic intentions for Burma, however, Aung San made contact with the British, who once again advanced into Burma, this time under the banner of the World War II Allied forces. Above, soldiers of the British Army advance through the streets of a Burmese town in January 1945.

After years of colonization, his country was about to earn its independence. While he reveled in his victory, Aung San did not know that a continent away, officials of the British government had conflicting opinions on the fate of Burma's political status.

FAMILY AND INDEPENDENCE

Initially, the British government did not intend to relinquish its colonial control over Burma. Aung San had to gather support from the people of Burma once again. In March 1946, he organized the first of two Panglong Conferences. There, representatives from several Burmese ethnic groups convened to discuss the future of the country. At the conference, Aung San emphasized that solidarity was crucial for any hope of independence. In his address to the members of the conference, he said that "the basis of a nation was not 'race or culture but a feeling of oneness that develops as different people share hardship and prosperity in common.'"[16]

Aung San came away from the conference with the unified support he needed to pressure the British. Initially, he was appointed deputy chairman of an executive council that included several members of AFPFL. After Aung San showed his independence from the communist faction within the ethnic leadership in Burma by expelling some communist sympathizers in the AFPFL, however, he was summoned to Great Britain to discuss the specifics of an independent Burma. On January 27, 1947, Aung San and Britain Prime Minister Clement Attlee signed an agreement that outlined the steps toward full independence within a year. In addition, plans were drawn up to hold elections for a constituent assembly before the arrival of summer.

It was Aung San who truly was the engineer of Burma's independence. There was still much work to do, however, to secure the cooperation of different groups who wanted certain provisions for their participation in establishing a new government. At the second Panglong Conference in February, Aung San said to those in attendance:

> The dream of a unified and free Burma has always haunted me. . . . We who are gathered here tonight are engaged in the pursuit of the same dream. . . . We have in Burma many indigenous peoples: the Karen, the Kachin, the Shan, the Chin, the Burmans and others. . . . In other countries too there are many indigenous peoples, many "races." . . . Thus "races" do not have rigid boundaries. Religion is no barrier either, for it is a matter of individual conscience. . . . If we want the nation to prosper, we must pool our resources, manpower, wealth, skills

and work together. If we are divided, the Karen, the Shan, the Kachin, the Chin, the Burman, the Mon and the Arakanese, each pulling in a different direction, the Union will be torn, and we will come to grief. Let us unite and work together.[17]

Aung San was working very hard to achieve a smooth transition from colonization to independence, often traveling around the country making speeches, listening to the concerns of the various groups within Burma, and working on the many details necessary to create a new government. Aung San was often accompanied on these trips by his wife, Ma Khin Kyi, and his children, two sons—Aung San U and Aung San Lin—and a daughter, Aung San Suu Kyi. The boys were four and three, and Aung San Suu Kyi was barely a year old.

The daughter of Burma's hero was born on June 19, 1945, just months after he led his BIA forces in the attack against the Japanese and drove them from the country. Aung San Suu Kyi represented the first children of a free Burma. At the time, Suu Kyi was too young to understand the significance of her father's remarkable achievements; that would come later in her life. For now, the petite girl with dark hair, dark eyes, and a smile like her father's, enjoyed the life of any small toddler with many privileges. As a result of her father's prominence in the country, the family's Sorrenta Villa in suburban Rangoon was rarely without visitors. Other politicians, representatives of the many ethnic groups, military advisors, and businessmen were all helping Aung San put together the plans for the establishment of the new government.

A HERO'S DEATH

On June 9, 1947, the Constituent Assembly convened for the first time. Aung San's longtime colleague and friend, Thakin Nu, was elected the Assembly's first president. Demonstrating the all-inclusive policy of the new Burma, three women were elected to seats in the Assembly. Aung San's AFPFL Party won 196 of the

Above, Burmese delegates in London for talks on Burma's independence pose with British officials in front of 10 Downing Street. From left to right, in the front row, they are U Ba Pe, Thakin Mya, Clement Attlee (the British prime minister), Aung San, and Tin Tut.

202 seats up for election. Unfortunately, Aung San would never get to see his beloved Burma complete the transition from foreign occupation to independence. On July 19, 1947, just one month after his daughter's second birthday, Aung San was assassinated while he was in an Executive Council meeting at the secretariat building in Rangoon. A group of heavily armed men rushed into the meeting and sprayed bullets everywhere, killing Aung San and several members of his Cabinet, including his oldest brother, Ba Win. In an instant, the 32-year-old leader of Burma's independence was gone. He left behind a stunned nation of free people, and a wife with three young children she would now have to raise

alone. Aung San Suu Kyi would never know her father, a hero in life, and now a martyr in death.

It was critical to keep the transition to independence moving forward, and so almost immediately after the assassination, Burma's British transitional governor, Hubert Rance, appointed Aung San's longtime colleague, U Nu, as prime minister. In the fall of 1947, the Constituent Assembly approved the constitution,

U Saw

Born in 1900 in Tharrawaddy, Burma, U Saw came from rather humble beginnings; however, he secured a license to represent clients in some legal cases and eventually went into politics. Early in his political career, U Saw attained recognition in Burma when he agreed to help with the legal defense of Saya San, the leader of the 1930–1932 rebellion against the British colonization of Burma. Although U Saw was not university educated, as were most of his Burmese political colleagues, this did not deter him from entering the political arena.

Fresh from his work on the Saya San trial, U Saw adopted the honorific title "Galon," after the name Saya San used for his army. Galon was a magnificent mythical bird in Hindu mythology that guarded the sky. In 1935, U Saw purchased *Thuriya* (The Sun), a nationalist Burmese newspaper that he used for self-promotion and as an outlet for his own political views. He was fascinated with Japan and visted the country that same year. He returned to Burma with a strong desire to model Burma's government after Japan's totalitarian regime. To this end, in 1938, U Saw founded the Myochit Party and fashioned a Galon army in the likeness of the storm troopers of Nazi Germany. Instrumental in helping to overthrow Burma's Prime Minister Ba Maw in 1939, U Saw served as minister of forests before becoming prime minister in 1940.

the first for the Union of Burma. Six months after Aung San's death, Burma was formally granted its independence. The official day marking self-rule was January 4, 1948. Burma was renamed the Independent Union of Burma. A short time later, an investigation uncovered evidence that pointed to rival U Saw as the one who planned the assassination. He was later tried, convicted, and executed for the murders.

In the early years of World War II, during a visit to London, U Saw failed to secure dominion status for Burma. Undeterred, he secretly met with the Japanese to obtain a deal with them, should they prevail in the war. When he returned to Burma, U Saw was arrested and sent to prison in Uganda for the remainder of the war. When he returned to Burma in 1945, he reestablished his Myochit Party, which was in strong opposition to Aung San's Anti-Fascist People's Freedom League (AFPFL). Aung San, in an attempt to unify all factions within Burma, allowed U Saw to accompany the Burmese contingent to London to work out the negotiations for Burma's independence. U Saw refused to sign the agreement because he thought that Aung San gave the British too many concessions.

In a last-ditch effort to derail the agreement, U Saw urged the Burmese to boycott the elections held on April 9, 1947. He was unsuccessful, and Aung San and the AFPFL achieved an overwhelming victory. To ensure that Aung San never took his place as prime minister of Burma, U Saw organized a band of gunman to assassinate Aung San and his ministers. On July 19, 1947, Aung San and members of his newly formed cabinet were gunned down in a conference room, while they planned the new government. It did not take investigators long to trace the purchase of the weapons used in the assassination to U Saw. He was arrested, tried, and convicted of conspiracy to commit murder. On May 8, 1948, U Saw was executed at Insein Prison and buried there in an unmarked grave.

Even though Aung San was gone, his countrymen would not forget him or let him be forgotten. In turn, his family, particularly young Aung San Suu Kyi, would always be reminded of Aung San and the sacrifices he made for them and his homeland. A city street bears his name, as does a market where everything from jewelry and clothing to handicrafts and food are sold. There is also the Bogyoke Aung San Park and Museum, situated on Natmauk Road. The museum was built on the grounds where Aung San and Ma Khin Kyi once shared a home in the 1920s. Perhaps the greatest honor bestowed upon Aung San, however, was the creation of a national holiday in his memory. Every year on July 19 at 10:37 A.M., sirens are sounded throughout the country, followed by two minutes of silence to honor the nine members killed that fateful morning in Burma's impending independence. The chance to know her father was taken away from young Aung San Suu Kyi, but there would always be reminders of him and the life he gave for Burma.

EARLY LESSONS

Even though Aung San was gone, those who had worked with him, respected him, and loved him remained a part of the family. Young Suu Kyi would learn the importance of duty to country and devotion to its very freedom from the many people within her country, as well as outside Burma, who would have an impact on her life. Of course, Aung San Suu Kyi's greatest role model was her mother. Although she had not played as visible a role in the quest for Burma's independence as her husband, Ma Khin Kyi had strongly supported Aung San and the efforts of the AFO. Many evenings, Ma Khin Kyi and the general opened their home to numerous colleagues, who came to plan and map out strategies for a postcolonial Burma.

Ma Khin Kyi was an educated woman who had attained a respected career as a nurse and midwife before she was married. She had also been active in the women's movement in Burma, joining the Women's Freedom League, a political group that was active in the independence movement against the British in the

1930s. Sharing her husband's passion and dedication to securing Burma's independence had earned Ma Khin Kyi the admiration and respect of the general's friends and colleagues. Aung San's sudden death left his seat in the parliament vacant. To continue to serve the people of Burma, Khin Kyi decided to fill her husband's seat in the country's new governing body. Known as a perfectionist and a highly disciplined woman, Khin Kyi exemplified the standard of conduct she expected of her children. Khin Kyi was also a compassionate woman and a devout Buddhist, and she never spoke of feelings of hatred or wanting revenge against her husband's assassins. These qualities would be the ones her daughter would embrace as she grew up.

Khin Kyi stayed in close touch with Aung San's many political and personal colleagues, to ensure that her children would always know what kind of man their father had been. Suu Kyi was almost constantly in the company of the people who had known, fought side by side with, and respected her father, and they happily shared stories of their experiences with the young girl. The exposure to so many educated, experienced, and dedicated adults had a great influence on Suu Kyi, one that contributed to her views about the world and helped shape her own beliefs and principles. Yet, not unlike most other children in her country, Suu Kyi and her brothers were raised in the traditional ways of the Burmese people. Respect, generosity, consideration, and benevolence to others, especially to adults, were all core values taught to every Burmese child, regardless of class or position in society.

Suu Kyi was also fortunate to have a large family support system. Grandparents, aunts, and uncles all lived nearby, and Suu Kyi always had plenty of company. She could play with her cousins on the grounds of the house, or learn from relatives about her Buddhist religion and the life of Buddha. Suu Kyi learned how to move within the world of Burmese women, often wearing the traditional *longyi* or ankle-length skirt and flowers entwined in her long, braided hair. She gained an appreciation for reading and loved to read mystery stories, especially ones that featured her favorite detective, Sherlock Holmes. She played with dolls, but she

Two-year-old Aung San Suu Kyi, bottom center, is pictured with her parents and two elder brothers, in 1947. Only a short time after this family portrait was taken, Aung San, Suu Kyi's father, was assassinated while he was in an Executive Council meeting.

also loved the freedom to run freely outdoors, playing soccer or exploring her surroundings.

Suu Kyi's favorite playmate was her older brother, Aung San Lin. The two were very close. They were often seen playing together on the grounds of the house, kicking a ball back and forth or engaging in some other game. One day, Lin dropped a toy gun they were playing with at the edge of the ornamental lake on the grounds and went back to retrieve it before he and his sister went home. According to Suu Kyi, he never returned.

It was discovered later that Aung San Lin accidentally drowned. Lin's death was a terrible loss for the family and hit seven-year-old Suu Kyi particularly hard. "His death was a tremendous loss for me. At that time I felt enormous grief . . . but it was not something

I couldn't cope with."[18] Suu Kyi also acknowledged that Lin's death in many ways affected her more than did her father's.

Upon learning of her son's death, Khin Kyi was as stoic as she had been after her husband's death. She had been at work and remained there until she finished what needed to be addressed that day before going home. Professional duties and responsibilities came before personal ones. Suu Kyi described her relationship with her mother as being very Burmese,

> which means mothers don't really discuss personal problems with their children. Parents don't do that in a Burmese context. There is a certain reserve between the generations. Mothers of my mother's generation just don't have heart-to-heart talks with their daughters.[19]

Suu Kyi's upbringing taught her to keep her emotions in check and to have self-control at all times. Khin Kyi taught her children the importance of serving others, as their father had. She also taught them the importance of standing up for what one believes in and not being a coward in the face of threat or adversity. Suu Kyi had always been afraid of the dark. She later recalled that she thought the fear stemmed from being terrified of ghosts. The Burmese are very fond of telling ghost stories, and Suu Kyi had heard her share as a youngster. Taking a lesson from her mother, Suu Kyi finally conquered that fear at age 12 by forcing herself to leave the safety of her room in the middle of the night to get a glass of milk while all alone in the dark. Once she was able to do that, she expanded her journey by wandering through the rest of the dark house until she no longer feared the dark.

Unlike most of her peers, Suu Kyi had been forced to learn how to cope with tragedy and loss at a very young age. Often, learning how to cope with adversity makes one stronger. Suu Kyi had a strong mother as her role model, and the values of her people's culture, instilled in her from a very young age, helped shape her character. These intangibles would only serve her well as she entered adulthood.

CHAPTER 5

International Education

During the time Suu Kyi was growing from child to adolescent to teenager, there was still much turmoil in the governance of Burma. It had always been difficult to unify the many different ethnic groups. The peoples of Burma speak more than 100 languages and belong to three major racial groups: the Mon-Khmers, the Tibeto-Burmans, and the Thai-Shans. In addition, there are seven groups of people, separate from the Burmese, that are large enough to have their own administrative states: the Chins, Kachins, Karen, Kayahs, Mon, Arakanese, and Shans. General Aung San had spent countless hours meeting with representatives of these various peoples to gain unification for an independent Burma. He was able to gain their initial cooperation, but it was a very fragile coalition, one that quickly deteriorated after January 4, 1948. Several rebellions left governmental control of the country limited to a small area beyond the capital city of Rangoon.

Despite the continued unrest among the peoples of the newly formed nation of Burma, Suu Kyi lived the life of a child of a national hero and politically engaged mother. In 1953, Ma Khin Kyi was appointed Burma's first minister of social welfare. During her tenure, she was active in establishing social welfare organizations to assist the many Burmese who were suffering from poverty and other difficulties. As a youngster, Suu Kyi probably did not realize just how much influence her parents had had on Burma's young independent history, but she certainly understood when years later she wrote of her parents:

> It has been said that Daw Khin Kyi, in marrying Aung San, married not a man only but a destiny. And Aung San had married a woman who had not only the courage and warmth he needed in his life's companion but also the steadfastness and dignity to uphold his ideals after he was gone.[20]

Suu Kyi's father had carved out a lasting legacy in his service to Burma. As Daw Khin Kyi became one of the most prominent woman politicians in Burma, Suu Kyi was very aware of what it meant to be dedicated to freedom and devoted to one's country. For a time, Suu Kyi was not a very disciplined student, wanting to play rather than to concentrate on her schoolwork, but as she matured, her grades reflected her intelligence and revealed a talent for languages. Although she was a practicing Buddhist, Suu Kyi attended the English Methodist High School, a private institution in Rangoon. Classes were taught in Burmese and English, and Suu Kyi did well with both languages. One of her teachers during that time taught a class on ethics, and it gave Suu Kyi a better understanding of the way other people and cultures formulate opinions and beliefs.

Life in India

In 1960, Ma Khin Kyi was appointed Burma's ambassador to India, which meant that the family needed to move to a new

(continues on page 46)

Influences on the Peacemaker

Aung San Suu Kyi has often said that the greatest influences on her life were her father, Aung San, and India's great leader, Mohandas Gandhi. "From Gandhi she drew her commitment to nonviolence, from her father the understanding that leadership was a duty and that one can only lead in humility and with the confidence and respect of the people to be led."*

From the time she was old enough, Suu Kyi learned all she could about her father. Once she saw the injustice in her country, she could not turn away from doing something to change it. At the rally at Shwedagon Pagoda on August 26, 1988, Suu Kyi said, "I could not, as my father's daughter, remain indifferent to all that was going on. This national crisis could, in fact, be called the second struggle for independence."** Aung San was assassinated just before he could assume his place as prime minister of the newly independent Burma. He was only 32 years old.

Once entrenched in the fight for freedom and democracy in Burma, Suu Kyi embraced many of Mohandas Gandhi's protest techniques in her own resistance movement against Burma's military junta. This rather frail-looking man, known as the Father of India, was a primary force behind freeing India's people from British rule through nonviolent resistance and civil disobedience.

One of the most revered spiritual and political leaders of the twentieth century, Gandhi was born in the port city of Porbandar, India, on October 2, 1869. Having studied law in London, Gandhi returned to India. He then accepted a job doing legal work in South Africa, another country under British rule. He remained in South Africa for two decades, working toward securing rights for India's people. During that time,

> he developed a method of direct social action based upon the
> principles of courage, nonviolence, and truth, called *Satyagraha.*
> He believed that the way people behave is more important than

what they achieve. Satyagraha promoted nonviolence and civil disobedience as the most appropriate methods for obtaining political and social goals.***

When Gandhi returned to India in 1915, he began to apply the tenets of Satyagraha to work on gaining independence for India. Though he was arrested many times for his protests and disobedience, he believed his was an honorable cause. One of his most effective techniques was to go on hunger strikes, sometimes bringing him close to death.

In 1947, India gained its independence from Britain. The former colony was partitioned into two independent nations, mostly Hindu India and Muslim Pakistan, resulting in riots between Hindus and Muslims. Gandhi had always espoused tolerance and began a campaign for a united India where Hindus and Muslims would learn to live in peace together. Instead, the division resulted in wide-ranging violence and bloodshed. Gandhi went on a fast and would only end it if opposition leaders promised to end the fighting. The fast lasted five days before Gandhi was given assurances from both sides. He was assassinated by a Hindu fanatic 12 days later. Gandhi remains one of the most respected and well-known figures in history.

---

*Abrams, Irwin. *Heroines of Peace: The Nine Nobel Women.* Antioch University September 22, 1997. Available at http://nobelprize.org/noble_prize/peace/articles/heroines/index.html.

**Kane, John. *The Politics of Moral Capital.* UK: Cambridge University Press, 2001, p. 148.

***Chew, Robin. "Mahatma Gandhi: Indian Spiritual/Political Leader and Humanitarian." 1995. Available at http://www.lucidcafe.com/library/95oct/mkgandhi.html.

(continued from page 43)

place. Suu Kyi, at 15 years old, would embark on a new adventure and live in another country. She and her brother, Aung San U, moved with their mother to New Delhi, the capital of India. Soon afterward, Aung San U went off to college in England, where he would study electrical engineering. Suu Kyi and her mother settled in "a large house in extensive grounds with a magnificent garden, housing meant for the most senior Indian officials and, as a special mark of esteem, offered to Daw Khin Kyi and maintained by the government as beautifully as in British days."[21]

Suu Kyi's life was just as busy in her new surroundings as it had been in Rangoon. They were living in a different country, but it was not a completely foreign one to Suu Kyi. India is a neighbor to Burma, and the two countries share both cultural and religious ties. There is also a large population of Indians living in Burma (approximately 2.5 million), so Suu Kyi was not unfamiliar with the culture of the people in her new environment. She continued her educational studies, first at the Convent of Jesus and Mary, an all-girls Catholic school, and then at Lady Shri Ram College for Women. For Suu Kyi, nonacademic time included a variety of activities, such as piano lessons and flower arrangement classes. Suu Kyi also took riding lessons, where she met other children whose parents were diplomats and Indian officials. These included the sons of future Indian Prime Minister Indira Gandhi and the grandsons of India's first prime minister, Jawaharlal Nehru. Now that she was a teenager, Suu Kyi was also mature enough to assist her mother with some of her duties as ambassador, which often included hosting diplomats and other political officials at their home.

Initially, Suu Kyi had not wanted to move to Delhi, because she did not want to leave the friends she had in Rangoon, but she soon made new friends in India and adjusted well. After school, lessons, and diplomatic engagements, she also found quiet time in which she could disappear into the world of books. Reading was one of Suu Kyi's passions. She still enjoyed a good mystery novel,

Above, American Olympic gold medalist Jesse Owens speaks at Delhi University in 1955. Only a few years later, Aung San Suu Kyi would begin her college education at the university.

but she had expanded her literary interests to include political philosophy and Greek mythology, as well as the writings of India's spiritual leader Mohandas (Mahatma) Gandhi. Gandhi was the pioneer of Satyagraha, which was described as "resistance through mass civil disobedience." Founded on *ahimsa,* or "nonviolence," Satyagraha became one of the foremost philosophies of freedom struggles worldwide.[22] Gandhi's leadership helped India gain its own independence from Britain. Suu Kyi was fascinated with Gandhi's teachings and read not only his writings but also those of the philosophers who had influenced him.

END OF DEMOCRACY

Suu Kyi had matured into a remarkable 17-year-old by the time she was ready to begin her college education. Ma Khin Kyi's friends and colleagues often marveled at how easily Suu Kyi navigated through conversations about politics and how she had already begun to form her own philosophies about life, truth, and people's moral principles and values. When she began her studies at Delhi University in 1962, her homeland was in turmoil. At the time, Suu Kyi could not have known how the changes occurring in Burma would eventually affect her. What she could see, however, was how those changes very much negated all the work her father had done in securing a free and democratic nation.

Since its beginning, Burma's government under U Nu had been rocky, because so many factions within the country wanted autonomy. The situation was so bad in the late 1950s that U Nu feared a military coup. To prevent this from happening, in 1958, he called on his former colleague from the Thirty Comrades and BIA, General Ne Win, to serve as interim prime minister to restore order and keep the country from plunging into a civil war. Addressing parliament, Ne Win said, "I promise to do my best to hold fair and free elections within six months, if the insurgency and crimes are brought to an end within that period of time."[23]

Though it was nicknamed the "caretaker government," in reality, Ne Win's administration looked less custodial and more iron-fisted in nature. A new cabinet was formed, and an ultimatum went out to the countless rebels causing the unrest: Surrender or face execution. Hundreds of politicians were also arrested, in an attempt to restore order throughout the country.

Although Ne Win did bring the country back under control, he also established the National Solidarity Association (NSA), which comprised mostly military personnel. Once order had been regained, Ne Win kept his promise and restored the civilian government by opening parliament up for elections in 1960, and U Nu was overwhelmingly reelected prime minister. The NSA was allowed to continue to exist, however. Ne Win did comply with his promise to restore free elections and a new parliament, but he had other, future plans for radical change.

On March 2, 1962, Ne Win wrested control of the government in a military coup. U Nu was arrested and sent to prison. Ne Win

In March 1962, General Ne Win led a military coup that overtook the Burmese government. Ne Win, pictured above in December 1962, then embarked on the formation of an oppressive new regime that expelled all foreigners from Burma and stifled all dissent.

cited a desire to establish a society that would benefit all peoples living in Burma, but he actually formed one of the harshest, most restrictive regimes in the world.

Ne Win began to isolate Burma from the outside world. With the formation of his new regime, all foreign citizens were expelled from the country. Banks, educational institutions, and all forms of communication fell under his control, and anyone who protested against the regime was arrested or beaten by the military. Burma had no hope of achieving the democracy that Aung San had dreamed of and died for. Now the Burmese had no voice, only a dictator who ruled through fear and intimidation. One of the few Burmese from U Nu's government to hold a post was Ma Khin Kyi. Although she disapproved of Ne Win's policies, she remained ambassador to India because she still believed she could better serve the people of Burma by staying than by resigning.

It wasn't long before Ne Win and his advisors began plunging Burma into poverty and desperation, for they knew little about how to operate the country on a day-to-day basis. Shortages in food, fuel, medicine, and other supplies changed the nation from one trying to grow and prosper to one of the poorest countries in the world.

LEARNING WESTERN WAYS

Suu Kyi wanted to learn more, and in 1964 she decided to follow her brother to England. She was accepted at England's renowned Oxford University, where she would continue to study philosophy and delve more into political science, the study of political institutions and behavior. Things in Burma had changed quite a bit since she had moved to India. Questions about Burma's future certainly had her mother concerned, but what could Suu Kyi do about the crisis unfolding back home? She would come to answer that question not as a 19-year-old college student, but as the grown daughter of the nation's hero.

For the first time in her life, Suu Kyi was going off on her own. She had been accepted at St. Hughes College, one of the five women's colleges that were part of Oxford University. Fortunately for Ma Khin Kyi's peace of mind, and to reassure Suu Kyi that she would never be totally alone, longtime family friends Sir Paul Gore-Booth (former British ambassador to Burma) and his wife,

Patricia, opened their home to her. She was invited to stay with them during school breaks and over holidays, when she could not make it back to India. Visiting with the Gore-Booths provided a window into the Western world that was unknown to Suu Kyi. People dressed differently and the food was different from what she had been accustomed to living in Southeast Asia. Suu Kyi was accustomed to eating dishes made with spicy curries over rice, vegetables, and lots of fish. Westerners ate eggs and bacon, with a diet that consisted of meat and vegetables such as potatoes.

At the time Suu Kyi attended Oxford, a cultural revolution was taking place in Europe and the United States. Teens were listening to rock and roll and had stopped wearing the more conservative clothes of the previous decade. They were dressing more casually, often in blue jeans and miniskirts. When Suu Kyi arrived on campus, she was still wearing her modest, traditional Burmese clothing. In the 1960s, there was a change in moral attitudes among the younger generation. It was a time in which people were freer to express feelings, and they shed more conservative, restrained behavior. Suu Kyi did not know of this world, having come from a society that was outwardly reserved and not freely expressive. There were campus parties that ran until late in the night. At most of these parties, alcohol flowed freely. Suu Kyi did not drink or smoke, so she spent the majority of her time consumed by her studies.

The lifestyle on campus was so alien to her initially that Suu Kyi rarely socialized with the other students. Soon, however, she made friends with those whose backgrounds were similar to hers—Indians, Africans, and even some British. She slowly learned about other ways of life and began to share her own customs and food preferences with her fellow classmates. Suu Kyi soon discovered that the best way to get around the St. Hughes College campus was on a bicycle. Not long after, she decided to wear jeans, as it was very difficult to ride a bicycle wearing the longyi. She also traded her long braids for one solid ponytail, but she continued to wear a flower in her hair, according to the Burmese custom.

BECOMING MORE WORLDLY

On school breaks, if Suu Kyi did not go back to India to visit her mother, she accepted the hospitality of the Gore-Booths and stayed with them. During one visit, she met a young British student who was a classmate of one of the Gore-Booth's children. Michael Vaillancourt Aris, who had been born in Havana, Cuba, was studying history and customs at the University of Durham, in London. His mother, Josette, was French-Canadian, and his English father, John, was an officer with the British Council (Britain's principal agency for cultural relations overseas).

According to Patricia Gore-Booth, Michael fell in love with Suu Kyi at that first meeting at their home. Michael's friends did not think Suu Kyi returned his feelings because the Burmese rarely looked favorably upon romantic relationships between people of different ethnicities. Suu Kyi surprised many people when she and Michael began to date. Although their schools were more than 60 miles apart, they managed to see each other quite often. They also began a written correspondence that helped them to maintain their budding relationship.

One summer, instead of heading back to India or staying with the Gore-Booths, Suu Kyi joined another family friend in Algeria, who was there working for the United Nations (UN). Ma Than E. was an old friend of the family; she knew Suu Kyi's father well from the time he had spent in London while negotiating Burma's independence. The general, as she referred to him, had made it a point to visit with all the Burmese—students, workers, and visitors—who were in and around the British capital. Ma Than E. had developed a deep respect for Aung San and Khin Kyi, and a special admiration for their daughter, Suu Kyi. Years later, she wrote of Suu Kyi, "[T]he firm roots of Suu's indomitable spirit and unusual personality lie in the ineffaceable memory of her father General Aung San and in her upbringing by her remarkable mother Daw Khin Kyi."[24]

Ma Than E. was in Algeria to establish a UN Information Centre in the newly independent country. Algerians had struggled through an eight-year battle for independence from their

French colonizers, and much of the country was in ruins. It was especially difficult to find housing for people coming into Algeria to help rebuild. Suu Kyi learned of one project to build homes for the widows of freedom fighters killed in the countless battles waged for independence, and she decided to volunteer. The experience was an extraordinary opportunity for Suu Kyi. She lived in a camp for several weeks, working side by side with other young, dedicated people from many countries, including France, Lebanon, Holland, and Germany.

When not working, Suu Kyi did some traveling to explore her surroundings. Her new Algerian friends took her to a wedding in the Kabylie Mountains in the northern region of Algeria. She also traveled to other parts of the North African region, including the Sahara Desert and an archeological site of Roman ruins. Although her time was limited, Suu Kyi also made visits to parts of Morocco and Spain.

Suu Kyi returned to Oxford to finish her studies, and she graduated in 1967 with a bachelor of arts degree in philosophy, politics, and economics. She and Michael had continued to date, and although the two were beginning to fall in love, Suu Kyi stayed in London for only a short time, teaching and doing research work. She wanted to continue her studies doing postgraduate work in New York City at New York University. Michael had made plans to stay at Oxford to continue his own studies, so the couple would now be a continent away from one another. Accustomed to being apart, Michael and Suu Kyi agreed to write often and telephone whenever possible. New York was going to be even more formidable than London had been, but Suu Kyi had a friend there awaiting her arrival. Ma Than E., the woman Suu Kyi affectionately called "Auntie," would be there to greet her Burmese friend when she arrived in America.

CHAPTER 6

Life of One's Choosing

Suu Kyi went to New York and moved into Ma Than E.'s apartment in midtown Manhattan. She pursued her postgraduate studies at New York University, where she met Ma Than E.'s friend, Frank Trager, a professor of international affairs. Trager had lived in Burma for several years and written *Burma: From Kingdom to Republic.* Since he had done a lot of traveling in the Far East and learned about the people and cultures of Southeast Asia, Trager was delighted to assist Suu Kyi with her studies.

Suu Kyi's bus rides back and forth from the apartment to New York University were real ordeals; she often found herself in the company of some of the city's rougher residents. After a short time, Ma Than E. suggested that Suu Kyi postpone her postgraduate work and consider a job at the UN. The headquarters of the world organization was only a five-minute walk from their apartment, and it would offer Suu Kyi exposure to the real political and diplomatic world, which she could never achieve from educational study alone. It was also an exciting time for Suu Kyi to be working at the

UN because of her Burmese nationality. The secretary-general, the UN's highest official, was Burmese. U Thant, the first Asian secretary-general of the UN, had been named to the position in 1961, after the organization's second secretary-general, Dag Hammarskjöld, died in a plane crash. U Thant was elected by the UN General Assembly in 1962, the same year Ne Win overthrew U Nu's democratic government in Burma, and U Thant would serve until his retirement in 1971.

Ma Than E. helped Suu Kyi get all the necessary paperwork in order to apply for the job. After going through the interviewing process and receiving stellar recommendations from some of the many prominent people she had already impressed with her poise, intelligence, and passion for knowledge, Suu Kyi was hired. She worked at the UN for three years, the last two spent as part of a small contingent whose primary job was to support the deliberations and activities of the Advisory Committee on Administrative and Budgetary Questions. As explained by Ma Than E. in *Freedom From Fear:*

> The members of this small, compact committee were appointed not as representatives of their countries but as experts on financial matters. The programmes and budgets of the United Nations and all its branches as well as all the Specialized Agencies, such as the WHO (World Health Organization) and the FAO (Food and Agriculture Organization), were submitted to this committee for appraisal, comment, modification and final approval. It was extremely hard work, but most interesting for its close examination of the financial implications of all UN activities, and for its members, people with quite exceptional minds.[25]

During Suu Kyi's free time in the evening or on weekends, she volunteered to read or visit with patients at New York's Bellevue Hospital. As Ma Than E. explained in Suu Kyi's book, *Freedom From Fear,*

[B]ellevue is mainly concerned with the city's poorest incurables and derelicts, who are brought in when life becomes too much for them, a temporary refuge for those on the verge of physical and mental collapse. Men and women are always needed to help with programmes of reading and companionship. Suu chose to volunteer many hours of her time every week for this. It was in the same tradition of service as her mother's.[26]

UN Secretary-General U Thant

The third secretary-general of the United Nations, U Thant, was born in Pantanwa, Burma (now Myanmar), in 1909. He also held other government posts and worked as an educator. By the time of his death in 1974 from lung cancer, he was greatly respected internationally.

Thant was the oldest child in a prosperous family. When Thant was only 14 years old, however, his father died, and the family struggled financially. Thant became a teacher at the National School and then at a young age became its headmaster. The local superintendent of schools, Thakin Nu (later referred to as U Nu), and Thant became good friends. Later, when the superintendent became prime minister of Burma, he asked Thant to work with him in the government as director of broadcasting. Over the years, Thant continued to

U Thant worked as the director of Burmese broadcasting under U Nu, as well as holding other government positions. In 1957, he became Burma's permanent representative to the United Nations; he was appointed to be UN secretary-general in 1961. Above, U Thant poses with U.S. president Richard Nixon in 1970.

During this time period, under Ne Win's regime, life for the Burmese people continued to deteriorate. The military used strong-arm tactics to silence opposition to the government. Ma Khin Kyi had retired to her home in Rangoon after her term of service was finished in 1967. She had been a vocal critic of the government, yet her standing in Burma as the wife of a hero made her untouchable. At worst, the officers and delegates in Ne Win's

work in the government, becoming U Nu's closest advisor and confidant. By 1957, he had become Burma's permanent representative to the United Nations.

Thant was unanimously appointed acting secretary-general of the United Nations in 1961, after the death of UN Secretary-General Dag Hammarskjöld. Then, in November 1962, he was again unanimously appointed, this time to the secretary-general position. He was reappointed for a second term in December 1966 and continued in the post until he retired in 1971. While he held the post, he gained wide recognition for his help in the Cuban missile crisis, and he was in charge of many successful mediation meetings. The U.S. government turned against him, however, when he criticized America's handling of the Vietnam War. Still, by the time of his retirement, he remained on speaking terms with all the powerful countries, something his two predecessors had not been able to manage. He tried to use Buddhist principles in his work and apparently these served him well.

When the military government then in power in Burma refused to hold any official ceremony for Thant or bestow upon him any honors upon his death, students took his coffin, buried him, built a temporary mausoleum, and led antigovernment speeches. Troops moved in, killed some students, took the coffin back, and reburied U Thant at the foot of the Shwedagon Pagoda. Angry citizens held riots in the street, and the government declared martial law. The events became known as the U Thant crisis.

U Thant's body remains at the pagoda. His memoirs were published posthumously in 1978.

cabinet might speak harshly to Ma Khin Kyi or to members of her family.

Suu Kyi received such treatment during a lunch she and Ma Than E. were invited to attend at the home of U Soe Tin, Burma's delegate to the UN. Several of Burma's ambassadors were also in attendance, including Burma's chief delegate, Colonel Lwin, who began to interrogate Suu Kyi about her continued use of her diplomatic passport even though her mother was no longer a member of Burma's political delegation. Not to be rattled, Suu Kyi handled herself calmly and politely, explaining that the regular passport was being held up in Rangoon, relieving the colonel's concerns that she might be taking advantage of her mother's past standing in the government.

Of course, Colonel Lwin would indeed check out the problem, but Suu Kyi had not offended or debated the situation with him or the others. The general feeling also was that, as the daughter of Aung San and Khin Kyi, Suu Kyi carried within her the same spirit and love of her country that her parents had.

A NEW CHAPTER

After living in the United States and working at the UN for three years, Suu Kyi decided that she was ready to marry and start a family; this took precedence over developing her career at the UN. Despite the thousands of miles that separated them, Suu Kyi and Michael Aris had maintained a relationship through very frequent letters to one another. During the time Suu Kyi was in New York, Michael had finished his educational studies at Durham University in London and then accepted a position as a tutor to the royal family in the Himalayan kingdom of Bhutan. After visiting with her mother in Burma toward the end of 1970, Suu Kyi decided to fly to Bhutan to see Michael before returning to her work in New York. Both knew they had fallen deeply in love, and Michael asked Suu Kyi to marry him. She accepted, and an engaged young woman returned to New York for her final year of work at the UN.

During 1971, Suu Kyi wrote many letters to Michael (187 letters over an eight-month period). Although she had no doubts that she loved Michael, Suu Kyi worried about her friends' and family's reaction to her marriage to a foreigner. Would they see this as a rejection of her Burmese heritage and her country? In the introduction to Suu Kyi's book, *Freedom From Fear*, Michael wrote that Suu Kyi expressed her concern that her family and friends might misinterpret their marriage and believe it to mean that Suu Kyi no longer carried the same devotion to her family and country. Suu Kyi knew in her heart that one day she would have to return to Burma, and she needed to know that she would have Michael's understanding and support. She asked only one favor of him:

> I only ask one thing, that should my people need me, you would help me to do my duty to them. Would you mind very much should such a situation ever arise? How probable it is I do not know, but the possibility is there.
>
> Sometimes I am beset by fears that circumstances and national considerations might tear us apart just when we are so happy in each other that separation would be a torment. And yet such fears are so futile and inconsequential: If we love and cherish each other as much as we can while we can, I am sure love and compassion will triumph in the end.[27]

Michael understood and promised to support Suu Kyi in whatever decisions she felt she might have to make should circumstances compel her to do so.

In a Buddhist ceremony on January 1, 1972, Michael and Suu Kyi married at the London home of the Gore-Booths. Together, they returned to Bhutan, where Michael continued his duties with the royal family. Bhutan had become a member of the UN in 1971, while Suu Kyi was still working there, and she was able to secure a job with Bhutan's foreign minister as a research advisor on UN policies. The couple's time in Bhutan was relaxed and exciting, as they settled into married life together. Their mood was captured in a snapshot taken during their explorations of the Himalayan countryside in their jeep with their terrier; the photo was included in letters sent to friends and family in London and Burma. That summer, Michael and Suu Kyi learned that they were going to be parents. Suu Kyi had wanted to start a family and eagerly awaited the arrival of her first child.

FAMILY FIRST

After a year in Bhutan, the couple returned to Britain, so that Michael could start his studies toward a doctorate degree at London University. They moved into a tiny apartment, where Suu Kyi spent the remainder of her pregnancy learning how to sew and experimenting with cooking a variety of foods. Michael and Suu Kyi's first child, a boy they named Alexander, was born in April 1973. In 1974, Michael became a junior research fellow at St. John's College and accepted a teaching appointment in Tibetan and Himalayan studies at Oxford University. The family moved into a tiny two-bedroom apartment in town. Living on a college professor's salary was a challenge, and the house was almost always full of people. Friends and family, including a beloved aunt of Suu Kyi's, came to visit often. There were also the university colleagues who came over and carried on academic discussions with Michael.

Suu Kyi had put her own studies on hold while she focused on her primary job as mother to Alex and wife to Michael. She loved her role, as family is always paramount to the Burmese people. The family's flat was on the ground floor of a house that had been converted into individual apartments. The front room was open and airy, with high ceilings and large windows that permitted the sun's rays to bathe the room in natural light. The back of the apartment, however, was small and cramped, even more so with their collection of books, baby furniture, and accessories.

Suu Kyi adjusted to and enjoyed the challenges that came with others depending on her. She spent some of her time mak-

Michael Aris and Aung San Suu Kyi pose in a photograph from the 1970s. Having met while Suu Kyi was studying at Oxford in the mid 1960s, the couple continued their courtship across oceans until their marriage in 1972.

ing curtains for the big bay windows in their apartment, grocery shopping, cooking, and despite a very tight budget, decorating the apartment to feel like home for her family. Suu Kyi did continue to read quite a lot while Alex slept, and she took a part-time job at the Oxford University library, where she catalogued the university's collection of Burmese books.

The arrival of a second child, Kim, in September 1977 made things both physically and financially even tighter for the Aris family. The couple managed in their cramped quarters until Michael received better financial compensation for his teaching duties. Soon after the raise, the family of four moved into a house in Park Town, "a then shabby-genteel nineteenth-century crescent curving elaborately round a quiet central garden, and ringed by unfrequented overgrown back lanes. The house was tall and narrow, the top three of its five floors initially occupied by sitting tenants."[28] The additional space was, however, quickly filled with a continuous stream of guests.

LOOKING OUTWARD AGAIN

Beginning to feel the need to expand her world again beyond Michael and the boys, Suu Kyi taught herself Japanese. She also embarked on a writing career that was sparked by a strong desire to know more about her father. She began writing about the general, and her first work, entitled *Aung San,* appeared in a series called *Leaders of Asia,* which was published by the University of Queensland Press in 1984. During this time, she also wrote a juvenile book called *Let's Visit Burma*, plus two others on Nepal and Bhutan in the same series for the Burke Publishing Company, in London.

As she learned about her father's early attempts at securing Burma's independence, Suu Kyi became fascinated by Aung San's initial ties with the Japanese. In 1985, she was offered a scholarship to the University of Kyoto. Going to Japan would allow Suu Kyi to research more about her father's time in Japan and his preparation for the march on Burma during World War II. Suu Kyi thought that perhaps she would even find a few former soldiers who might be able to share some of their personal recollections, as well. Kim went with his mother to Kyoto, while Alexander went with his father to India, where Michael had accepted a fellowship at the Indian Institute of Advanced Studies at Simla. In 1987, Suu Kyi finished her research in Kyoto. She accepted her own fellowship as a visiting research scholar at the Indian Institute, where Michael was engaged in his studies. She and Kim left for India, and the family was reunited.

In the Aris-Kyi family, each member had the freedom to explore and pursue his own interests, and at the same time, Michael and Suu Kyi maintained a truly loving marriage, where both participated in raising their sons. Although Suu Kyi was married to a foreigner, she made sure her sons knew the traditions and heritage of the Burmese people. Alex and Kim were taught the Burmese language and raised in the Buddhist religion. During a visit to Burma in 1986 with their grandmother, Khin Kyi, both Alex and Kim participated in the traditional Buddhist ceremony of initiation into monkhood. This important ceremony was held at Khin Kyi's home in Rangoon, a high honor for her, and a joyous celebration for Suu Kyi and the boys. Suu Kyi tried to give her sons the most expansive exposure to other cultures, languages, and ways of life. In all respects, the boys were typical of youths elsewhere. Alex developed an interest in sports and, like his mother, loved to study philosophy. Kim had a general affection for reading books on a variety of topics and he liked to play the guitar.

In 1987, while still on her fellowship in India with Michael and the boys, Suu Kyi had to take a hiatus in her work to make a trip to London, where her mother had just undergone cataract surgery. Ma Khin Kyi was doing well and received many cards and letters from the friends and colleagues she had cultivated over the years. Her son, Aung San U, now living and working in California, surprised his mother and came for a visit during her recuperation. After recovering in London for a few months, Khin Kyi returned to Burma, and Suu Kyi returned to her family in India.

Michael, Suu Kyi, and the boys moved back to London in September, so Michael could return to his academic life at Oxford. Suu Kyi wanted to continue with her own studies, so she enrolled at the London School of Oriental and African Studies, where she began to work on a doctoral thesis on Burmese literature.

RETURN TO A VOLATILE HOMELAND

The repressive military regime ruling Burma had continued to feed a simmering unrest among the people, which was ripe for eruption. Most of the visible unrest was coming from Burma's young—students who were protesting the government's repressive control over a country that was in deep economic decline and suffering from shortages of food and other resources. One writer described the environment:

> There were many kinds of restrictions on every aspect of life. They even have to buy/sell rice in black market. We had to depend on black market goods from Thai, Indian and Chinese borders. There was no production in our country. There was no future for us. The number of unemployed was high. Our country was that dark and with lost future. It was a spark of light: that was 13 March 1988.[29]

On the eve of March 13, a small student protest at the Rangoon Institute of Technology turned deadly. Riot police sent to the institute immediately clashed with students. Ko Kyaw Htin witnessed the beginning of the riot:

> Just after nine, a friend of mine came to pick me up. He told me that people were throwing stones at each other. There was a town and gown brawl. With the spirit of a young person, I joined them. We chased them and they retreated and the like in the BPI road. Then, the "Lon Htein" riot police arrived. And 5–6 fire engines also arrived. By that time, the students and the civilians were already kept separately. The riot police were placed in the middle, and the civilians were in the alley and we were in our campus. We told our professor U Tin Tun Aung and the like to enter the campus. We entered the campus. U Tin Tun Aung and the like were hit by some stones thrown from the civilians, maybe. We started to disperse. At around 9:45–10 A.M., they started to fire us with tear gas and guns.[30]

Another eyewitness, Ko Aung Din, described what happened after the tear gas was unleashed:

The situation was quite ugly. At the time, balls of smoke bombs dropping down on us with bangs. The smoke rose up and the whole place became dark and only then did we realise that we were hit by tear gas. Smoke got into our eyes. Thus, we were all falling down and then we heard the sounds of gunfire went "bang, bang." We all ran away. Then, we regrouped among the pillars of the main campus. Everyone was wounded more or less. Some people were crying. There were three students with bullet wounds. Up till then, I have never seen any one with gunshot wounds in my life, except in movies. Now, I saw those gaping gunshot wounds of my friends in front of me. They were Ko Phone Maw, Ko Soe Naing and Ko Myint Oo.[31]

When the siege ended, one student was dead and many more were injured. The brutality and protests continued for several days, but the events of March 13 marked the beginning of what would become a nationwide uprising for freedom and democracy to return to Burma.

Back at Oxford, the last night of March had, for the Aris family, been much like most other evenings. Both Alexander and Kim were in bed, and as Michael later recalled, he and Suu Kyi were also in bed, reading. The ringing of the telephone broke the peaceful silence in the house. It was a call for Suu Kyi from Burma. Her mother had suffered a severe stroke. As soon as the call ended, Suu Kyi began to pack. As Michael watched his wife prepare to leave to be with her mother, he had a premonition that their lives were about to change forever. Two days later, Suu Kyi was at her mother's side at the hospital in Rangoon, thousands of miles away from her husband and sons, and the home she had made with them. London could never be her true home, however; her home was and always would be the land of the pagodas, the country of its hero, her father, Aung San.

CHAPTER 7

8-8-88

When Suu Kyi arrived at the hospital in Rangoon to be with her mother, in many ways, the news was not good. Ma Khin Kyi's stroke had been severe, and the prognosis for her recovery did not look good. Suu Kyi came home to a country that was worse than it had been in some time. Under the repressive and at times brutal governance of Ne Win's regime, the country had suffered economically, politically, and socially. The quality of life of most Burmese people was abysmal. Ne Win had been in power for 26 years, and in that time he had taken Burma from a position as one of the richest countries in Southeast Asia to that of one of the poorest. His regime had successfully isolated Burma from the outside world, limited the flow of information about its corrupt governance beyond its borders, and continually violated its people's most basic human rights.

Ne Win's brand of government demonstrated his serious lack of understanding and expertise in running a country. In 1987, when Burma's economy plunged to the lowest it had been since the 1950s, he devised a plan to combat the hyperinflation. According to daughter

Sandar Win, Ne Win's astrologers advised him to change Burma's monetary system by replacing all the country's bank notes with bills divisible by the number nine. Why? Because nine was Ne Win's lucky number! Under Ne Win's new monetary system, millions of Burmese suddenly found themselves bankrupt—the money they had saved was no longer worth the paper on which it was printed.

The Burmese people awoke each morning to a vision of a country that was crumbling, decaying, and dying before their eyes:

> The disparity between rich and poor is found throughout the country, with the majority of the population living in terrible squalor, without proper food, sanitary conditions, shelter, or medical care. Basic services in Rangoon, however, are equally inefficient for everyone. Even in the best hotels the tap water is undrinkable, the plumbing barely functions, and electricity is grossly inadequate for the massive construction that is going on. . . . As for paved roads, the surfaces usually crack within months under the heat of the scorching sun, leaving gaping holes and causing numerous traffic accidents.[32]

Suu Kyi knew conditions in Burma were not the best, but she had not lived on a daily basis in the midst of such deplorable conditions. She had captured snapshot glimpses during brief visits, alone or with her family. Rangoon and her country did not much resemble the home she had left 28 years before.

Quiet resignation by the Burmese people over unsatisfactory living conditions began to give way to vocal disapproval of the regime. Protests sprang up on college campuses and in the streets of Rangoon and other cities around the country. The military did what any dictatorship would do: It tried to silence the discontent before the rebellion could throw Burma into complete anarchy. A riot outside a tea shop on the Rangoon Institute of Technology campus, on the night of March 13, ended in but one of many violent crackdowns by the regime. In another appalling incident where the military showed its utter disregard for life, 41 students

Above, demonstrators gather in Rangoon on August 6, 1988. When Aung San Suu Kyi returned to Rangoon in April 1988, she had heard about the unrest, but her primary concern was to care for her ailing mother.

who had been rounded up and arrested for disorderly conduct suffocated while being held in a police van.

CARETAKER AMID UNREST

Although Suu Kyi had heard about the violence in Rangoon before her arrival in April, her primary focus was on her mother's health rather than on the surrounding unrest. While Khin Kyi remained in the hospital for three months, Suu Kyi was at her bedside, hoping for some sign of her mother's improving health. There was none forthcoming, and when it was apparent that the hospital staff could do no more for her mother, Suu Kyi decided to take Khin Kyi home. She wanted her mother to be in familiar surroundings and to live her remaining days in a peaceful and loving environment. When the school semester ended, Michael, Alex, and Kim flew to Rangoon to be with Suu Kyi and Ma Khin Kyi. The presence of her grandsons lifted Khin Kyi's spirits, and she did improve for a brief time. Michael and the boys were not surprised that Khin Kyi's home was orderly and serene, a result of Suu Kyi's firm but loving guidance.

Outside the family compound, the environment was anything but serene and peaceful, however. By July, it was apparent to Ne Win that the internal chaos that was spreading each day could not be squelched by mere military force. Calling for an emergency session of his parliament, Ne Win surprised everyone when he used the platform to announce his decision to step down from his post as chairman of the BSPP. In his speech, Ne Win took indirect responsibility for the country's current unrest and recent bloody events. Although he also recommended that a referendum be held to decide Burma's future, he quickly added an ominous message in his speech to those choosing to demonstrate:

> Although I said I would retire from politics, we will have to maintain control to prevent the country from falling apart, from disarray, till the future Organizations can take full control. In continuing to maintain control, I want the entire nation, the people, to know that if in future there are mob disturbances, if the army shoots, it hits—there is no firing into the air to scare. So, if in the future there are such disturbances and if the army is used, let it be known that those creating disturbances will not get off lightly.[33]

In his introduction for Suu Kyi's book, *Freedom From Fear*, Michael Aris recalled watching Ne Win's extraordinary and surprising speech before the congress on the state-controlled television with his wife. Along with the rest of Burma's people, Suu Kyi was electrified at the prospect that the nation would finally be able to control its own destiny.

To many, Ne Win's speech did not sound like someone retiring, but rather someone who would continue to make party policy and decisions from behind the scenes. On July 27, General Sein Lwin succeeded Ne Win as the head of the BSPP. Nicknamed the "Butcher of Rangoon," Lwin's appointment earned a swift and unfavorable reaction; many of Burma's citizens felt he had been responsible for the deaths of several demonstrators during the March riots. Further inflaming the situation, the BSPP rejected Ne Win's call to hold a referendum on whether Burma's people preferred the one-party system of government already in place or a change to a multiparty system of government.

AT THE STROKE OF 8

No one could have prepared themselves for what took place just days after Ne Win's departure. Enraged by Sein Lwin's refusal to allow the people of Burma once again to have a say in their governance, demonstrations in the streets escalated to grand proportions:

> On August 8, 1988, a day known in recent Burmese history as the "Four 8s," a nationwide strike was called that included students, civilians, lawyers, doctors, monks and civil servants. Convinced that the resignation of Ne Win meant that Burma would finally be liberated from one-party rule, crowds surged into the streets in a euphoria of countrywide prodemocracy demonstration.[34]

The response from Sein Lwin made the demonstration response in March look like a skirmish by comparison.

The day began peacefully and full of optimism for those who participated in the strike demonstration organized by the All Burma Students' Democratic Front. Around 8:00 A.M., thousands of unarmed protestors from Rangoon's various townships— North Okkalapa, South Okkalapa, Thaketa, Thingangyun,

Yankhin, and Bahan—came into the streets and began to march peacefully toward City Hall. There was a sea of people marching in columns, carrying banners representing the townships from which they came, visible in the massive crowd. The throng of people grew as it made its way closer to the center of Rangoon. The crowd eventually merged with the thousands awaiting them at Bandoola Park, in front of City Hall. There were other marches held throughout the day in most of Burma's major cities. Some, looking to America's democracy as a symbol of hope, gathered outside the U.S. Embassy. One student remarked, "It was an incredible moment in our lives. We so desperately wanted freedom and democracy. The moment had come when we thought it would be possible to come out from under the boot of military oppression that had trampled us since we were young children."[35]

General Sein Lwin responded to the outpouring of Burma's people onto the streets by deploying thousands of troops all across Rangoon and into the countryside. The demonstrators could see the armed troops, ominously waiting but restrained in their behavior. The above student described the continuing scene, saying that the demonstrators knelt down in front of the soldiers and sang to them, telling them that they only wanted democracy and freedom. The soldiers waited until 11:45 P.M., then hell rained down on everyone. The troops aimed their weapons into the crowd and opened fire on the unarmed men, women, and children who had gathered around City Hall. This action commenced a four-day massacre that littered the streets and sidewalks of Burma with bodies.

The same student described the almost indescribable:

> They had orders to fire and they did. Many students, some friends, and some of my family members were shot dead on the spot. We had no idea that our own people would kill us. There was blood everywhere. Loud screams and the cracking of gunfire echoed loudly. People began falling down everywhere.[36]

The killing was not just confined to the protestors, nor did the soldiers demonstrate any civility or compassion:

> On August 10, troops fired in front of Rangoon General Hospital, killing doctors, nurses, and Red Cross workers and wounding others who were pleading with them to stop. Injured victims were denied medical care. Eyewitnesses describe soldiers entering the crowded emergency room at Rangoon General and shooting students on stretchers and in hospital beds. In North Okkalapa, a suburb of Rangoon, bodies were thrown into trucks and taken to Kyandaw Cemetery, where live students were cremated along with the dead. Soldiers blindly carrying out the orders were convinced by their superiors that the students were "communist insurgents."[37]

Although there are no official numbers, it is estimated that between 3,000 and 10,000 people were killed. The massacre was reported on television stations and radio networks all over the world. Sein Lwin had lived up to his nickname. He resigned on August 12 and was replaced by Dr. Maung Maung on August 19. The horrific violence of the 8-8-88 Massacre unified the citizenry of Burma even more. The country seemed poised to succeed in overthrowing the one-party BSPP dictatorship and finally forming a democracy in Burma.

SYMBOL OF HOPE

Aung San Suu Kyi, together with family and friends of her mother's, watched the August events unfold from Khin Kyi's University Avenue home. Khin Kyi's health did not improve, even under the loving care of her daughter. Many of those who knew her, and those who had worked with her and her husband, came to the house to pay her a visit out of respect and friendship. Some of those who came to visit were still politically active and interested in seeing democracy return to Burma. One was U Nu, the former Burmese prime minister and comrade of General Aung San, who had been overthrown during Ne Win's military coup and placed in "protective custody" for four years. Another was a former Burmese patriot, U Tin Oo, who joined the Burmese Army as a 16-year-old in 1943 and later served as Minister of Defense under Ne Win. In 1980, he had retired to a quiet, private life, after being imprisoned for four years on suspicion of treason, but the events of those days in August prompted him to pay a visit to Khin Kyi's home.

The fact that Suu Kyi was in Burma was slowly becoming known in certain political and diplomatic circles. It was hard to maintain a low profile for the daughter of a national hero, as Suu Kyi indeed was. Michael Aris described the scene at 54 University Avenue:

> In the nationwide turbulence which followed Ne Win's resignation on 23 July 1988 and the immediate refusal by his party to agree to a referendum on Burma's future, Suu's house quickly became the main center of political activity in the country and the scene of such continuous comings and goings as the curfew allowed. Every conceivable type of activist from all walks of life and all generations poured in. Suu talked to them all about human rights, an expression which had little currency in Burma till then. She began to take her first steps into the maelstrom beyond her gates.[38]

When Suu Kyi got off the plane at Rangoon Airport five months earlier, she had no political aspirations beyond trying to get several libraries under way as a means of honoring her father's memory. The stream of visitors who came to see her and to discuss starting a movement to bring democracy back to Burma gave her the first true glimpse into what her father had really meant to the people of Burma. She explained,

The advantage of being somebody in a democratic party is that you don't really have to prepare yourself as an individual for such responsibility because you are not going to be a dictator. You are going to be working as part of a team. Although Aung San died, the independence to which he had dedicated his life came to his country. . . .[39]

Although a life in politics held no attraction for Suu Kyi, she agreed to make some overture to the BSPP, thus beginning her first political initiative. In an open letter entitled "The Formation of a People's Consultive Committee," dated August 15, Suu Kyi wrote to Thura U Kyaw Htin, Secretary of the Council of State of Burma. In the opening statement of the appeal, Suu Kyi wrote:

The people of the country, both *sangha* and laity, should live peacefully within the framework of the law and should submit to the government their just aspirations by peaceful means . . . a special request has been made to the Government to fulfill as far as possible the people's lawful aspirations.[40]

Suu Kyi went on to propose the creation of an independent committee to act as an intermediary between the students and the government to oversee a national election. In that election, people should be permitted to form political parties and all that went with it, including choosing candidates and electing new representatives for the creation of a new government. The letter went unanswered. On August 24, Suu Kyi made an appearance in front of Rangoon General Hospital to announce that she would be addressing a rally at the Shwedagon Pagoda two days later.

On August 26, like her father had 41 years earlier, Suu Kyi gave a speech on the steps of the sacred Shwedagon Pagoda. Accompanied by her husband, Michael, and sons Alex and Kim, Suu Kyi took her place on the shrine steps. To an estimated crowd of more than half a million people, Suu Kyi spoke of what she felt were the three most important topics: the absolute necessity for nonviolence, a return to human rights, and democracy for Burma. Suu Kyi answered those who questioned why she, who had lived abroad and was married to a foreigner, was getting involved in Burma's political chaos. She explained that although those facts were correct, they did not affect her love for and devotion to her country. Even though she would have liked to stay away from power politics, she explained why that was no longer an option for her and why she was choosing to be a part of the democracy movement now: "The answer is that the present crisis is the concern of the entire nation. I could not as my father's daughter remain indifferent to all that was going on. This national crisis could in fact be called the second struggle for national independence."[41]

Suu Kyi's speech, in which she invoked her father's work, patriotism, and desire for a free and democratic Burma, was an emotional and yet powerful unifying message to her fellow countrymen. As the daughter of Aung San, not only was she a moving reminder of the Burma that once was, but also the living symbol of hope for the future for all of Burma's people. The beginning of Suu Kyi's political involvement also marked the time when she had to say goodbye to Michael and the boys, as the start of the fall school term beckoned them back to England. As Michael said farewell to his wife, he was reminded of the promise he had made to her 16 years earlier, in which he told her that he would support her decision to help her country if that time ever came. Although Michael always believed that one day that time would come, he had imagined that it would happen later in their lives, when the boys were grown and off creating their own lives. He wrote: "But fate and history never seem to work in orderly ways. Timings are unpredictable and do not wait upon convenience."[42] Suu Kyi chose to step into the Burmese national crisis, and life for the Aris family was forever changed by that decision.

CHAPTER 8

Personal Sacrifice for Sake of Country

General Saw Maung quickly and stunningly ended the move toward the realization of democracy in Burma on September 18, 1988, with the seizure of power in a military coup d'état. With Saw Maung in power, a new party was established, named the State Law and Order Restoration Council (SLORC). Maung and the SLORC promised the Burmese people that free and fair elections would be held in 1990. In the meantime, law and order was the first priority in securing the safety and peace of the country. This meant he had invoked martial law: No more than four people were permitted to gather, or they would be imprisoned; any form of public demonstration was banned; it was forbidden to criticize the SLORC; military tribunals (which are often conducted in secret) would be used in place of civil courts; all media was to be put under the control of the state; and a nighttime curfew was imposed throughout Burma.

Suu Kyi and others with close ties to her in the freedom movement knew that the SLORC had no intentions of holding free and fair elections, now or ever. Still, in keeping with the promise of

In 1988, the National League for Democracy was founded and registered in order to take part in the elections sponsored by the SLORC. Above, the vice chairman of the NLD, U Tin Oo, stands with Aung San Suu Kyi as she speaks outside of her home in 1996.

holding such elections, on September 24, the National League for Democracy (NLD) was founded by U Tin Oo, U Kyi Maung, and Suu Kyi and registered with the SLORC election committee. Several hundred other parties also registered, including the All Burma Federation of Students Union (ABFSU) and U Nu's League for Democracy and Peace (LDP). Despite the ban on gatherings of more than four people, Suu Kyi began campaigning around Burma, talking about the need for reform in Burma's government and for turning the country into a free and democratic nation.

DEATH AMID CONFLICT

Politics had to be set aside when Ma Khin Kyi passed away on December 27. More than 20,000 people came to the house on University Avenue to express their condolences to Suu Kyi and her family. Michael and the boys flew in for the funeral, as did Suu Kyi's brother, Aung San U. With her nine-month struggle at an end, Khin Kyi's death actually brought a temporary unity to the country that it had not witnessed in a very long time. The SLORC cooperated with Suu Kyi as she made arrangements for the funeral of her mother, the wife of Burma's hero, Aung San.

Surprisingly, the SLORC, out of respect for Aung San's widow, even announced that all Burmese people, in spite of the ban on gatherings of more than four, could attend Khin Kyi's funeral freely and without the threat of retribution. Soldiers, students, and political leaders all came en masse to pay their respects. It is estimated that more than 100,000 people attended the funeral, including diplomats and dignitaries representing countries from all over the world. Thousands lined the streets from Khin Kyi's home to the Shwedagon Pagoda to watch the funeral procession that took her body to its final resting place.

As soon as the funeral was over, however, the SLORC went back to its thug tactics: emptying streets of demonstrators with gunfire, banging down doors of targeted dissenters in the middle of the night and dragging them off to jail, all the while continuing publicly to promise free elections and an orderly transfer of power to a newly elected civilian government. The SLORC considered Aung San Suu Kyi and her NLD Party to be particularly worrisome. Suu Kyi, through visits and speeches to dozens of cities and towns across Burma, had gained quite a following and support for the NLD Party. The SLORC used contradictory tactics where members of the NLD were concerned. Although they encouraged political parties to declare themselves openly, they imposed severe restrictions on speech and the freedom to assemble. Many "violators" of the laws were arrested and sentenced to prison without even having a trial.

The SLORC particularly targeted members of the NLD, but they never moved against Suu Kyi directly. They did, however, attack her character, raising questions about her motives and dedication to the Burmese people. They accused her of being a tool for the communists, who would take over the country. They questioned her patriotism, reminding her followers that she had married a British citizen and had made her home in England, not in Burma. Whenever Suu Kyi arrived to talk to a gathering of people, military jeeps would get there just ahead of her arrival. Using bullhorns, the soldiers in charge would warn the crowd not to listen to what Suu Kyi had to say. Many also believed that the man behind the formation of the SLORC was BSPP leader Ne Win. He had always considered himself Aung San's heir, despite the facts that U Nu was appointed to take hero's place when he was assassinated, and that Ne Win had harbored strong ill feelings against Aung San's party and its members.

FROM DANGER TO HOUSE ARREST

Suu Kyi was emboldened, not frightened, by the SLORC's harassment, and she even began to invoke Ne Win's name in her speeches. The harassment and defamatory comments about Suu Kyi only strengthened her resolve and brought her more supporters. It was a great risk for people to attend one of her appearances, as it violated the ban on meetings and put them at risk of arrest or imprisonment. Suu Kyi was also always at grave risk. Occasionally in her speeches, she almost sounded like she was taunting the SLORC, while seeking reconciliation with them. In one speech her words were aimed directly toward the SLORC leadership:

> To resolve problems . . . we must meet face to face. Why do you not have the courage? Why do you still hold the gun? . . . [If the leaders of the SLORC are not] willing to engage in dialogue, they are not fit to run a government, not fit to administer the nation. . . . Solving problems by using lethal weapons on unarmed civilians is a fascist method.[43]

Above, Aung San Suu Kyi gestures while speaking at a rally in 1989. Suu Kyi campaigned for election around the country, a move that made her a target of suspicion for the SLORC, eventually leading to her detainment under house arrest.

Almost fearless in her speeches, Suu Kyi privately knew there was always the danger that she could be harmed or arrested. On April 5, 1989, Suu Kyi and several of her supporters came very close to knowing the wrath of the government she criticized. While walking down a road in the village of Danubyu on their way to make a campaign appearance, Suu Kyi and her party were suddenly confronted by a military jeep full of soldiers. The soldiers jumped out of the vehicle and got down in a crouched position. Then, acting on the orders of an army captain, they aimed their rifles at Suu Kyi and the others. During the count-down to fire their weapons, Suu Kyi waved off her supporters and continued to walk down the road. Just before they were to begin shooting, an army major stepped in and ordered the soldiers to stand down. Suu Kyi had almost been assassinated, yet she later explained her actions by saying that she felt it was simpler to give the soldiers a lone target instead of involving everyone else.

Over the next few months, there were a few other occasions when Suu Kyi was in harm's way or could have been killed. At one memorial rally held in June for dissidents killed in the 8-8-88 Massacre, Suu Kyi and several students were fired upon. One person was killed. A planned memorial in early July was cancelled for fear of a bloodbath. And on July 19, while Suu Kyi was preparing to attend a memorial service to honor her father on the anniversary of his assassination, the SLORC took control of the ceremonies after they learned that she planned a particularly powerful and incendiary speech against the regime. She refused an invitation by the SLORC to join them and instead said she would attend separately.

Finally unwilling to tolerate Suu Kyi's soaring popularity and the powerful momentum her opposition party was enjoying, the SLORC moved against her. On the morning of July 20, "eleven trucks of armed troops rolled down University Avenue, blocking off either egress, as well as preventing anyone from leaving or entering Aung San Suu Kyi's compound."[44] There were many people inside the house, including U Tin Oo, U Kyi Maung, and Win Htein. Also during this tense time, Suu Kyi's sons Alex (now 16) and Kim (now 12) had flown to Burma to spend their summer school break with their mother. They, too, were inside the house. Michael had not yet arrived because he was attending his uncle's funeral in Scotland. Nothing more happened until late afternoon. Around 4:00 P.M., several soldiers and a few government authorities entered the house. The soldiers cut telephone lines and began searching the house for incriminating documents because Suu Kyi was the general secretary of the NLD. While the house was being searched, the officers accused Suu Kyi of being a dangerous subversive and endangering the state. Although she was not formally charged with anything, the authorities officially placed Suu Kyi under house arrest, cutting off any communication with the outside world. Under martial law, which had been invoked the evening before, the SLORC said they could detain any individual for up to three years without filing any charges or holding a trial. Suu Kyi could remain under house arrest for as long as the three-year period.

Several of Suu Kyi's associates were arrested, including Win Htein, who spent over five years in Insein Prison. NLD Party leader U Kyi Maung issued a statement about Suu Kyi's arrest, saying, "Aung San Suu Kyi's detention clearly shows that there is absolutely no democratic rights or basic human rights in Burma under the SLORC."[45] Kyi Maung was arrested shortly afterward and also imprisoned at Insein. For the SLORC, the arrest of members of the NLD Party was a systematic means to disable their greatest political rival. Years later, when confronted about Suu Kyi's house arrest, the SLORC justified their actions, explaining that Suu Kyi had greatly benefited by not being formally charged and held over for trial. Had that been the case, she would have been tried for treason, which automatically carries the penalty of death. They believed that Suu Kyi kept herself under house arrest to draw attention to her plight because she had grown bored with her mundane life in England.

Michael arrived at Mingaladon Airport in Rangoon to a military "welcome." He was surrounded by troops as soon as he disembarked from the plane and was whisked away without a trace. For 21 days, no one on the outside knew where Michael had been taken; he just disappeared. After gaining assurances that he would not talk to anyone connected to politics, the soldiers took Michael to the house in Rangoon. Michael and the boys stayed for three weeks and left for England on September 2, 1989. When they got home, the Burmese Embassy informed Michael that his sons' Burmese passports were no longer valid and had been cancelled because they were not entitled to Burmese citizenship status. When they left their mother in September, they did not know at the time that they would not see her again for six years.

During her detention, Suu Kyi did not know what would happen from one day to the next. Her opposition tried to make her marriage and motherhood an issue, leaking reports that her marriage was not as solid as it appeared; that she was more concerned about the children of Burma than about her own two sons; that having been given the opportunity to leave Burma and go back to her husband and family, she refused because they were not as important to her as was the cause of freedom and democracy for Burma. The SLORC even used Michael as a pawn to try to get Suu Kyi to leave, by permitting him to visit his wife without her knowledge ahead of time. Suu Kyi greatly resented the way Michael was used and insisted that he stay at her aunt's house on the grounds until they agreed to keep her informed of any visitors permitted to see her. To Suu Kyi, it was ludicrous for the SLORC to believe that trying to drive her out of her own country was an acceptable resolution to her. She was determined to show them that what they were doing to her was having no effect; her one and only concern was what they were doing to her nation and its people.

Suu Kyi passed the hours of total isolation by keeping a very orderly, regimented schedule. She would rise each day at 4:30 A.M. and begin her meditation. Left with a radio that was the only link to the outside world, Suu Kyi would listen to the BBC World Service, Voice of America, the Democratic Voice of Burma, and occasionally to a French radio station to keep up with the language. Radio time consumed about five or six hours of her day. She would also exercise to keep her body in shape, then bathe, eat breakfast, do some household chores, listen to music or play the piano, tend to her garden when it wasn't raining, and read. One staff person was permitted to bring Suu Kyi food, and when money became scarce, she sold her furniture with the help of the staffer to get money to buy everyday necessities. When she could, Suu Kyi spoke to the hordes of armed guards that surrounded her house. They, in turn, tried to make her a nonperson. They removed the number address from her house and changed shifts every eight hours to ensure that none of them would be influenced by Suu Kyi's point of view.

An avid reader since her youth, Suu Kyi spent many hours reading books from her mother's extensive library collection.

There were biographies on famous people such as Nehru and Mother Teresa. She read books on philosophy, politics, and her favorite topic, mysteries and detective stories. Cooking was always a challenge, since food was a scarcity in her home. Sometimes she would have fruit and tea or milk. It was a luxury to have a hard-boiled egg on the weekend. Over time, the garden became overrun with weeds, food was hard to come by, and Suu Kyi began selling off her mother's furniture in order to buy food and pay for electricity. Eventually she sold everything except the bed, the dining room table, and the piano. Some days, she was so weak from lack of food that she could barely get out of bed.

Suu Kyi spent some time writing to Michael and the boys, but she eventually put a stop to all correspondence because the SLORC was using the letters and packages received as propaganda against Suu Kyi; they reported to the citizens of Burma that while they suffered, she was living well as a prisoner and receiving luxury items like lipstick. As the months passed quietly, Suu thought about her sons and husband, but she never dwelled on her situation because she felt there was nothing she could do about the current circumstances. She leaned heavily on her faith in the teachings of Buddha and never hated her captors. She also never felt fear and said,

> Fearlessness may be a gift but perhaps more precious is the courage acquired through endeavor, courage that comes from cultivating the habit of refusing to let fear dictate one's actions, courage that could be described as "grace under pressure"—grace which is renewed repeatedly in the face of harsh, unremitting pressure.[46]

CLAMP DOWN

Although unable to help because of her house detention, Suu Kyi could only wait and see what happened with the coming of the elections in May 1990. The SLORC did carry them out as promised, but they were very unhappy with the results. Even though they forced Suu Kyi's name off the ballot because of her arrest status, it did not lessen her influence in the elections. The NLD Party won 392 of the 485 National Assembly seats, which was about 60 percent of the vote. The SLORC only received about 25 percent of the vote and won a mere 10 seats. The SLORC did not honor the results of the election, which would have ousted them from power. They stated that the elections were not intended to choose political leaders, but simply to elect representatives to a national convention that would be charged with the responsibility of writing a new constitution. They were swift to clamp down on any possible reprisals. All relevant NLD members who had not escaped were arrested and imprisoned. The results of the elections were denied, and Aung San Suu Kyi was still under house arrest.

To consolidate power, in 1991, the military bulked up its capabilities by purchasing $1.2 billion worth of military hardware from China to add to their 11 Soviet-made jets, 100 tanks, and various antiaircraft guns, assault rifles, and gunboats. Then the SLORC's army went on a rampage throughout Burma. Thousands of Burmese fled to neighboring countries while the soldiers literally burned villages to the ground, killing livestock, raping women, and murdering people for no reason. Land mines scattered throughout the countryside maimed hundreds of children who thought they were toys. Members of various ethnic groups were seized and placed in fenced-off areas at military camps. Reports of torture camps reached beyond Burma's borders, and the country was soon labeled a terror state.

THE NOBEL PEACE PRIZE

While Suu Kyi was in Burma, Michael had a collection of his wife's essays and some of the contents of her letters to him published in a book called *Freedom From Fear*. Although Suu Kyi had initially reacted negatively to the publication because of privacy concerns, royalties from the sale of the book provided

Suu Kyi with desperately needed money to sustain herself while she was under house arrest. Every time she was up for release, the SLORC would renew her confinement by changing the law. In July, Suu Kyi received her first international honor of that year. She had been chosen as the 1991 recipient of the Sakharov Prize for Freedom of Thought, which was awarded annually by the European Parliament. In honor of Russian dissident Andrei Sakharov, the award is presented to "honor individuals or organizations for their efforts on behalf of human rights and fundamental freedoms and against oppression and injustice."[47]

History of the Nobel Peace Prize

The awarding of an annual prize for peace was the idea of the scientist and inventor Alfred Nobel, who was born in Stockholm, Sweden, on October 21, 1833. When Nobel died in 1896, his will specified that a significant portion of his fortune should be dedicated to the creation of five prizes (a sixth, for economics, was added in 1969), including one for peace. Nobel stipulated that the peace prize be given to the person who had done "the most or best work for fraternity between nations, for the abolition or reduction of standing armies, and for the holding of peace congresses." Nobel also specified that, unlike the other prizes, which were to be awarded by Swedish committees, the prize for peace was to be awarded by a committee of five people elected by the Norwegian *Storting* (Parliament).

The first Nobel Peace Prize was awarded in 1901 to joint recipients Frédéric Passy and Jean Henry Dunant. Passy was leader of the French peace movement and main organizer of the first Universal Peace Congress. Dunant was the founder of the International Red Cross.

Over the years, the Nobel Peace Prize has been awarded to both organizations and individuals. The first organization was the Institute for International Law, honored in 1904 for its efforts to come up with the general principles that would form the science

On October 14, Suu Kyi was awarded perhaps the most prestigious honor by the Nobel Academy. Only the seventeenth individual and the eighth woman to be awarded the Nobel Peace Prize, Aung San Suu Kyi now captured worldwide attention. Upon announcing Suu Kyi's selection, Norwegian Nobel Committee head Francis Sejersted said that her struggle had been "one of the most extraordinary examples of civil courage in Asia in recent decades."[48] Suu Kyi was now in the company of such distinguished winners as Mikhail Gorbachev, the Dalai Lama, Elie Wiesel, Desmond Tutu, and Mother Teresa.

of international law. The International Committee of the Red Cross received the prize twice—in 1917 and 1944, for its efforts to promote international solidarity and brotherhood in the midst of war. The Office of the United Nations High Commissioner for Refugees received the prize in 1954; other organizations to receive the prize included the United Nations Children's Fund (UNICEF) in 1965, the Friends Service Council in Britain/American Friends Service Committee (1947), United Nations Peacekeeping Forces (1988), International Physicians for the Prevention of Nuclear War (1985), and *Médécins sans Frontières* (Doctors Without Borders) in 1999.

Over the years, the award has highlighted the achievements of men and women from many different nations who represent widely varying backgrounds and experiences. It is interesting to note that one of the people most closely identified with nonviolence, Mohandas Gandhi of India, never received the Nobel Peace Prize, despite five nominations. Suu Kyi is one of only 12 women to receive the Nobel Prize—a group that also includes Bertha von Suttner (1905), Jane Addams (1931), Emily Greene Balch (1946), Betty Williams and Mairead Corrigan (1976), Mother Teresa (1979), Alva Myrdal (1982), Rigoberta Menchú Tum (1992), Jody Williams (1997), Shirin Ebadi (2003), and Wangari Maathai (2004).

Suu Kyi made history, of sorts, by being the first recipient selected while in captivity. The SLORC's response to the news was that they would give no special treatment to their detainee-guest. They did announce that Suu Kyi was free to go to Oslo to accept her award, but Suu Kyi was smart enough to know that it also meant that she would not be permitted to return to Burma. Instead of risking permanent exile, Suu Kyi asked Michael and the boys go to Norway to accept the award on her behalf. On December 10, 1991, Alex and Kim jointly accepted their mother's award, as Michael proudly looked on. Francis Sejersted gave the gold medal to Alex, then 18, and the diploma to Kim, who was just 14. Sejersted praised Aung San Suu Kyi for her courage and her ideals. The 1,500 people in attendance gave the Aris family a standing ovation and deafening applause. It was Alex who read his mother's speech and said that his mother's quest for peace and democracy is basically a spiritual one. He also reminded each guest that each of us has a responsibility to one another. As his mother had often said, "To live the full life, one must have the courage to bear the responsibility of the needs of others . . . one must want to bear this responsibility."[49] No one there on that day, in that place time, could doubt that about Suu Kyi.

CHAPTER 9

The Lady

A side from the enormous prestige and publicity that comes with being awarded any of the Nobel Prizes (physics, chemistry, physiology or medicine, literature, economics, and peace), there is also a large monetary award that varies from year to year. Suu Kyi's Nobel Peace Prize came with a $1.3 million award. Yet, despite her own dire financial situation, she chose not to keep the money for herself. Instead, she announced that the money would be used to create a health and education trust for the Burmese people. Not wanting their very public detainee to suffer from ill health or malnutrition, the SLORC offered Suu Kyi money to help her buy food and other necessary items. Determined to take nothing from her captors, Suu Kyi refused. In time, with the proceeds coming in from *Freedom From Fear,* Michael was able to send his wife some money. Soon, Suu Kyi was able to eat better and regain her strength.

Suu Kyi won the Nobel Peace Prize at a time when democracy movements were taking shape on many continents, including Latin America, South America, and Africa. Since Suu Kyi had been awarded the peace prize, much more attention was focused on Burma and the repressive SLORC regime. The regime now had unwanted publicity for their human rights violations; their use of brutal and often deadly force to suppress any expression of opposition to the government; and their refusal to implement any reform or to honor the 1990 elections.

Instead of opening a dialogue with Suu Kyi and the NLD, however, the SLORC became even more repressive and restrictive. The SLORC began to close access to University Avenue more often, which kept people from visiting with Suu Kyi from across the yard. They also began to limit her opportunities to leave the house as well as ending her weekly gate-side meetings with soldiers or supporters. Every measure the SLORC took to minimize the visibility of "the Lady," as she had come to be called, increased her popularity and made those in the prodemocracy movement more determined.

LIFE IN DETENTION

Although her detention should have been based on a finite period of time, Suu Kyi believed that her detention was open-ended, left to the will of the government. At the same time, she firmly believed that Burma would eventually achieve democracy. After all, how long could a country keep its people repressed? Suu Kyi knew that the Burmese people most certainly did not have the basic human rights spelled out in the UN Declaration of Human Rights. They did not have the following human rights: They were not born free and equal in dignity and rights; they were not safe from being enslaved; they were not protected from being subjected to torture or to cruel, inhuman, or degrading treatment or punishment; they did not have the right to recognition everywhere as a person before the law; and they were most certainly not protected from being subjected to arbitrary arrest, detention, or exile. These human rights were only a few of the 30 articles stipulated in the UN document. It could only be a matter of time before external pressure from the international community, sanctions imposed on Burma by the UN Security Council, and perhaps most important, the unwavering will of the Burmese people would ultimately bring about change.

The Nobel Prize had given Suu Kyi some power over the SLORC. They were trying to figure out how to rid themselves of the martyr they created, and Suu Kyi was determined that they could not take away her rights. The SLORC had tried to appeal to Suu Kyi's family ties, offering to end her detention by giving her the opportunity to leave Burma and rejoin her family in England. In such a case, she would never be permitted to return to her native homeland. As the mother of two teenage boys, who at the same time felt an unwavering duty to country, this was an impossible choice. To arise each day to ask oneself the question: Do I choose freedom or confinement? Do I choose to see my sons, who live comfortable lives, or stay to help the people who are far less fortunate than them? How does anyone come to reconciliation?

In Suu Kyi's mind, there was never any question of leaving. Said Suu Kyi, "I know that whatever sacrifices my family and I have to make are very small compared to the troubles and uncertainties suffered by those of my colleagues who have not the protection of a famous father and international recognition."[50] The separation from their mother seemed more difficult for Alex than for Kim, however. Alex was the quieter, more introspective of the two and seemed to have trouble coping with his mother's house detention, a friend of the family observed. Kim, on the other hand, was in a rock band, had long black hair, and seemed to take his mother's work in stride.

Many leaders, artists, human rights advocates, and organizations began to call on Burma to release Suu Kyi from her detention. In April 1992, the SLORC regime had a change in leadership. Citing health reasons, Saw Maung stepped down from his position as chairman of SLORC, prime minister, and military commander-in-chief. His replacement, General Than Shwe,

(continues on page 94)

Critics of the Peacemaker

The military junta governing Myanmar are the obvious critics of Aung San Suu Kyi, her prodemocracy work, and her determined insistence that the military regime honor the results of the 1990 election. When Suu Kyi was awarded the Nobel Peace Prize in 1991, she was in the third year of house arrest imposed by the State Law and Order Restoration Council (SLORC). Even at that time, just a few years into championing the cause of freedom and democracy, Suu Kyi had captured the world's attention. Many in the global community echoed the sentiments of the Norwegian Nobel Committee, who said of her,

> Suu Kyi's struggle is one of the most extraordinary examples of civil courage in Asia in recent decades. She has become an important symbol in the struggle against oppression. [The] Committee wishes to honour this woman for her unflagging efforts and to show its support for the many people throughout the world who are striving to attain democracy, human rights and ethnic conciliation by peaceful means.*

Those who work towards freedom and democracy around the world, including former UN secretary-general Kofi Annan, support Suu Kyi's efforts. However, those who oppose her views, primarily the State Peace and Development Council (SPDC) of the Union of Myanmar, have a different perception of Aung San Suu Kyi, one that does not include the self-sacrificing devotion to her country and its people. Her detractors have argued that Suu Kyi was long ago transformed into a Western woman, having gone to school in England, worked in New York, and married a British citizen. She spent many years away from Burma, living in Europe while raising her children and pursuing her own academic interests. She was not actively involved with the goings-on in her homeland.

High-ranking members of the SPDC have often questioned her motives. Former SLORC/SPDC General Khin Nyunt explained the regime's stance:

Aung San Suu Kyi did not lead a normal life in accordance with our religious teachings and customs and traditions. Unfortunately, she is not leading the life of a normal citizen today because she is trying to cause political confusion and instability and unrest when we finally have peace and tranquility in the country... Frankly, if Aung San Suu Kyi had come back and worked for the country and married a Myanmar citizen, she might have been able to become a national leader.**

In the regime's view, Suu Kyi cannot understand the problems of her countrymen, having all but abandoned her country to create a life a continent away. According to them, she is actually doing more harm than good to the people of Myanmar by creating an atmosphere of confusion and instability. The regime has also accused Suu Kyi of being a tool of the communists. Said Colonel Hla Min, "The Communist Party cells saw her as a great advantage because she is the daughter of our national hero. They believed that if they could push her into the front and take advantage of her position, it would serve their purposes."*** Given what that the international community knows of the military junta's many human rights violations and iron-fisted rule, most consider the regime's statements about and against Suu Kyi to be nothing more than propaganda. The regime, however, is still in control of the country, and continues to punish Suu Kyi's defiance and activism. As such, the SPDC did not support her selection as a Nobel Peace Prize laureate.

---

*The 1991 Nobel Peace Prize: Laureates. The Norwegian Nobel Committee, Press Release. Available at http://nobelprize.org/nobel_prizes/peace/laureates/1991/press.html.

**Victor, Barbara. *The Lady,* p. 32.

***Ibid., pps. 34–35.

(continued from page 91)

although also an old protégé of Ne Win, seemed more liberal in his governance over Burma. He released several political prisoners, lifted the evening curfew, reopened some of the universities that had been shut down since the 8-8-88 Massacre, and even relaxed some of the restrictions imposed on Suu Kyi. He was the man who later changed the name of the country from Burma (its British colonial name) to Myanmar. In the beginning of 1993, Shwe ordered that a new national constitution be written. He was the leader with whom Suu Kyi would be trying to establish a dialogue now.

CALLING FOR RELEASE

In February, six Nobel Peace Prize laureates—Mairead Corrigan and Betty Williams (1976), Adolpho Pérez Esquivel (1980), Desmond Tutu (1984), Oscar Arias Sánchez (1987), and the Dalai Lama (1989)—attempted to visit with Suu Kyi but were denied entry into Burma. They went instead to the refugee camps along the Burma-Thailand border and saw the atrocities the SLORC military had committed against its people. Appealing to the international community to cease any and all relations with the Burmese government, they also called on the military junta to release Suu Kyi. According to Oscar Arias Sánchez, former president of Costa Rica, "Having been brutally denied her rightful place to be an elected leader of her people, Aung San Suu Kyi remains courageously committed to the principles of freedom and democracy . . . . She continues to inspire the people of Burma."[51]

In 1994, the junta started to show signs that they might release Suu Kyi. The country was in better economic shape than it had been for many years, and the SLORC did not want condemnation by any human rights or other groups to harm their situation further. For the first time since her arrest, the Lady was permitted visitors other than her family. U.S. Congressman Bill Richardson led a group that included Jehan Raheem, a representative from the UN and Philip Shenon, a reporter from the *New York Times*. During her three-hour visit with the delegation, Suu Kyi made it clear that gaining her release meant nothing if the SLORC did not publicly recognize the results of the 1990 elections and turn power over to those who had been freely and fairly elected to serve the people of Burma. Unfortunately, SLORC Intelligence Chief General Khin Nyunt made no concessions to Congressman Richardson. On his way out of Suu Kyi's home, Richardson noticed several banners with words written in Burmese that were attributed to Suu's father, Aung San. The congressman asked about one specifically, which Suu Kyi translated for him. It said, "You cannot use martial law as an excuse for injustice."[52]

The call for Suu Kyi's release would not die down. On July 20, a day after her fifth year in detention, activists, friends, and colleagues held rallies and vigils around the world on her behalf. U.S. President Bill Clinton said,

> I urge the Burmese military regime to heed the will of its own people by releasing unconditionally Aung San Suu Kyi. . . . I also call on the regime to honour the results of the 1990 election. . . . The regime should begin a substantive dialogue with Aung San Suu Kyi aimed at achieving a political settlement.[53]

Dr. Sein Win, prime minister of the exiled National Coalition Government of the Union of Burma, stated,

> The military regime thought that physical confinement would break her will . . . and that the people would forget her. . . . She remains strong, courageous and defiant as ever. . . . Recently, General Khin Nyunt disclosed that he wishes to hold talks with (her). . . . To prove that they are sincere . . . [she] should be released immediately.[54]

The U.S. Committee for Refugees released the following statement:

SLORC has now held Nobel Peace laureate Aung San Suu Kyi under house arrest for five years. And for more than four years, SLORC has effectively held democracy itself under house arrest in Burma. . . . The U.S. Committee for Refugees once again calls on the SLORC to unconditionally release Aung San Suu Kyi.[55]

FREE TO WHAT END?

Another year passed by slowly for Suu Kyi. Approaching her sixth year of detention, Suu Kyi did not think there was any reason to believe the SLORC would release her. Without warning, on the afternoon of July 11, 1995, a government car pulled up in front of University Avenue, which was still blocked off from the public and surrounded by razor wire, like a prison. Colonel Kyaw Win, SLORC's deputy chief of military intelligence, had come to inform Suu Kyi that her house arrest had ended and her freedom was being reinstated without any restrictions. Although she realized that nothing had changed to bring the NLD and SLORC any closer to reconciliation, Suu Kyi was now free to walk outside her home, free to talk to people again, free to go wherever she pleased. Soon, crowds began gathering outside the house. Suu Kyi went out to greet her supporters. A few days later, Suu Kyi spoke of her hope for a dialogue with the SLORC that would bring them all to some sort of agreement. Suu Kyi told the crowd, "I have always believed that the future stability and happiness of our nation depends entirely on the readiness of all parties to work for reconciliation."[56]

The intent of the SLORC was only to get Suu Kyi out of the spotlight. Over the past few years, they had been meeting at a national convention to rewrite the country's constitution. Although it had representation from various political groups within Burma, the SLORC had majority control. They had already accepted guidelines that would provide them with the leading role in governing Burma, and they had adopted policies that would make it impossible for Suu Kyi to hold elected office. Suu Kyi was not initially aware of the SLORC's plans, and she spent the early part of her freedom just reacquainting herself with life beyond the walls of her compound. Michael, Alex, and Kim flew to Rangoon, and they had a joyous family reunion. The visit was too brief, however, for the boys needed to return to England for the start of school. They did not know it would be the last time the family would ever be together again.

By early fall, it was apparent that the SLORC did not intend to have a dialogue about reconciliation, the return of human rights, honoring election results, or any other topic falling under the umbrella of democracy. Instead, they attacked Suu Kyi in the newspapers, raising questions about her true motives, accusing her of being a communist, having been married to a foreigner, and having moved away from her people and her country. Stymied by the SLORC's refusal to meet with them, Suu Kyi and the rest of the NLD leaders decided to announce a boycott of the convention. SLORC responded by expelling the 86 NLD representatives. They also began to arrest known NLD party members. Suu Kyi and other NLD members, as well as anyone who came to hear Suu Kyi speak, were in constant danger. Often at rallies, soldiers turned water hoses on the crowds, arrested people who planned to attend meetings, and frustrated Suu Kyi in any travel she attempted beyond Rangoon (now called Yangon). Suddenly Michael, Alex, and Kim were not permitted to come to Myanmar. A resigned Suu Kyi said, "Nothing has changed since my release. Let the world know we are still prisoners within our country."[57]

The more Suu Kyi spoke out against the SLORC, the greater their retaliation against her and the NLD. Hundreds of members were arrested; in 1996, she was again forbidden to give public speeches at the gate of her home. Soldiers, armed and threatening, shadowed her wherever she went. In 1997, SLORC changed its name to the State Peace and Development Council (SPDC), in an attempt to soften its image around the world.

In September 1999, while under house arrest, Suu Kyi made an address in a home video (screen grab above), which was smuggled from Myanmar to London. In the video, Suu Kyi granted her support to unilateral economic sanctions against Myanmar as a means of influencing the Burmese government.

They continued to try to attract foreign investment dollars, so Suu Kyi spoke out to dissuade foreign companies from investing in Myanmar, citing forced labor, corruption, and the fact that the money would only make it into the hands of a very few rich military leaders. Foreign investment would not do anything to help the people of Burma. Myanmar was also considered an exotic place to vacation, with its many pagodas, shrines, and statues. Tourism dollars were a good source of revenue for the junta. Suu Kyi asked people to boycott travel to Myanmar. She wanted to get at the heart and soul of the junta's economic prosperity.

THE COST OF THE STRUGGLE

Suu Kyi had, on a few occasions, come dangerously close to being hurt—or worse—in her pursuit of bringing freedom to the people of Burma. On June 28, 1998, she was injured when the military attacked a crowd of university students who had gathered at her home. She was detained by soldiers twice while attempting to leave Yangon to meet with members of the NLD. One of the standoffs lasted 13 days. Undaunted, and unafraid for her own safety, Suu Kyi kept the word out in the world that the junta was still repressing its people and refusing to make any concessions.

While Suu Kyi was facing these dangers, Michael was back in London fighting his own battle. He had not seen his wife since the brief time right after she was freed in 1995. Diagnosed with prostate cancer, Michael was told that the disease was too advanced to treat beyond keeping him comfortable. Despite numerous requests to visit Myanmar in order to spend time with his wife while he was still able to travel, Michael and the boys were refused entry into the country. The SPDC, however, strongly encouraged Suu Kyi to go to England to be with her dying husband in his time of need. Suu Kyi knew if she left, she would never be allowed to return to Myanmar. As difficult a decision as it was, Suu Kyi believed that Michael would understand. She stayed in Yangon. On his fifty-third birthday, March 27, 1999, Michael died in England. Although his sons were with him, his wife had to bear her loss alone in Yangon.

Suu Kyi worked through her grief by throwing herself into winning the struggle for democracy. There were many more standoffs with soldiers, some lasting hours, others lasting days. Suu Kyi was determined to keep spreading the word and attempting to gain support, and the SPDC was just as determined to stop her by any means necessary. Finally, when she tried to board a train to travel to northern Mandalay in 2000, Suu Kyi was again placed under house arrest. Ninety-two members of the NLD were detained, as well. While in detention, Suu Kyi was honored with

Because the government of Myanmar detained Aung San Suu Kyi, her sons often were called upon to accept awards in her name, including the Nobel Peace Prize. Above, son Alexander accepts the U.S. Presidential Medal of Freedom on her behalf from President Bill Clinton during ceremonies on December 6, 2000.

the highest civilian award by the United States, the Presidential Medal of Freedom. Alex accepted the award from President Bill Clinton on his mother's behalf.

For the next two years, interventions from representatives of the UN, the European Union, and the United States attempted to break the deadlock between Suu Kyi and the SPDC. A breakthrough came when Suu Kyi was again released from house detention on May 6, 2002. Suu Kyi explained what she thought was a factor in her release: "The fact that people in our country do want change. And that it is better for us to be on good terms than to be on bad terms. I would like to give the regime the benefit of the doubt, and I would like to believe that they genuinely want to do what is good for the country. And they see that reconciliation is the best thing possible that can be done."[58] Still, there was no move from the SPDC to allow free elections to take place or to adopt any other prodemocracy policies in Myanmar.

On May 30, 2003, while she was on a month-long tour in the north, a confrontation erupted when a pro-junta crowd stopped Suu Kyi's motorcade just outside the village of Depayin, near Mandalay. Officials were unsure how many people were killed in the resulting clash. Suu Kyi was taken into "protective custody," and no one saw or heard from her for several days. Finally, UN special envoy Razali Ismail was permitted to see her. He later reported that she was unharmed and otherwise healthy, but was still wearing the clothes she had on when she was arrested.

Upon learning of Suu Kyi's arrest, response from the international community came quickly. Secretary of State Colin Powell wrote in a *Wall Street Journal* op-ed piece,

> The junta that oppresses democracy in Burma must find that its actions will not be allowed to stand. . . . Their refusal of the . . . rights of Aung San Suu Kyi and her supporters could not be clearer. Our response must be equally clear if the thugs who now rule Burma are to understand that their failure to restore democracy will only bring more and more pressure against them and their supporters.[59]

Before she was returned to her home in Yangon, Suu Kyi spent some time in the hospital to undergo surgery. Suu Kyi's term of house arrest was set to expire on May 27, 2006, but the government extended it for another year, despite a direct appeal from Kofi Annan, the UN secretary-general at the time. At the time of this writing, she remains under house arrest. Now in her

60s, she is just as firm in her resolve to gain freedom and democracy for her country. Although there are continued calls for her release, they go unheeded. So, in her aging home in Yangon, Aung San Suu Kyi continues to lead the struggle for her country. She has never given up hope of having an honest dialogue to achieve reconciliation. Suu Kyi has said, "The only thing I have refused is to discuss leaving the country."[60]

Nobel Prize Acceptance Speech
Delivered on behalf of Aung San Suu Kyi, by her son, Alexander Aris

Your Majesties, Your Excellencies, Ladies and Gentlemen,

I stand before you here today to accept on behalf of my mother, Aung San Suu Kyi, this greatest of prizes, the Nobel Prize for Peace. Because circumstances do not permit my mother to be here in person, I will do my best to convey the sentiments I believe she would express.

Firstly, I know that she would begin by saying that she accepts the Nobel Prize for Peace not in her own name but in the name of all the people of Burma. She would say that this prize belongs not to her but to all those men, women and children who, even as I speak, continue to sacrifice their well-being, their freedom and their lives in pursuit of a democratic Burma. Theirs is the prize and theirs will be the eventual victory in Burma's long struggle for peace, freedom and democracy.

Speaking as her son, however, I would add that I personally believe that by her own dedication and personal sacrifice she has come to be a worthy symbol through whom the plight of all the people of Burma may be recognised. And no one must under-estimate that plight. The plight of those in the countryside and towns, living in poverty and destitution, those in prison, battered and tortured; the plight of the young people, the hope of Burma, dying of malaria in the jungles to which they have fled; that of the Buddhist monks, beaten and dishonoured. Nor should we forget the many senior and highly respected leaders besides my mother who are all incarcerated. It is on their behalf that I thank you, from my heart, for this supreme honour. The Burmese people can today hold their heads a little higher in the knowledge that in this far distant land their suffering has been heard and heeded.

We must also remember that the lonely struggle taking place in a heavily guarded compound in Rangoon is part of the much larger struggle, worldwide, for the emancipation of the human spirit from political tyranny and psychological subjection. The Prize, I feel sure, is also intended to honour all those engaged in this struggle wherever they may be. It is not without reason that today's events in Oslo fall on the International Human Rights Day, celebrated throughout the world.

Mr. Chairman, the whole international community has applauded the choice of your committee. Just a few days ago, the United Nations passed a unanimous and historic resolution welcoming Secretary-General Javier Pérez de Cuéllar's statement on the significance of this award and endorsing his repeated appeals for my mother's early release from detention. Universal concern at the grave human rights situation in Burma was clearly expressed. Alone and isolated among the entire nations of the world a single dissenting voice was heard, from the military junta in Rangoon, too late and too weak.

This regime has through almost thirty years of misrule reduced the once prosperous "Golden Land" of Burma to one of the world's most economically destitute nations. In their heart of hearts even those in power now in Rangoon must know that their eventual fate will be that of all totalitarian regimes who seek to impose their authority through fear, repression and hatred. When the present Burmese struggle for democracy erupted onto the streets in 1988, it was the first of what became an international tidal wave of such movements throughout Eastern Europe, Asia and Africa. Today, in 1991, Burma stands conspicuous in its continued suffering at the hands of a repressive, intransigent junta, the State Law and Order Restoration Council. However, the example of those nations which have successfully achieved democracy holds out an important message to the Burmese people; that, in the last resort, through the sheer economic unworkability of totalitarianism this present regime will be swept away. And today in the face of rising inflation, a mismanaged economy and near worthless Kyat, the Burmese government is undoubtedly reaping as it has sown.

However, it is my deepest hope that it will not be in the face of complete economic collapse that the regime will fall, but that the ruling junta may yet heed such appeals to basic humanity as that which the Nobel Committee has expressed in its award of this year's prize. I know that within the military government there are those to whom the present policies of fear and repression are abhorrent, violating as they do the most sacred principles of Burma's Buddhist heritage. This is no empty wishful thinking but a conviction my mother reached in the course of her dealings with those in positions of authority, illustrated by the election victories of her party in constituencies comprised almost exclusively of military personnel and their families. It is my profoundest wish that these elements for moderation and reconciliation among those now in authority may make their sentiments felt in Burma's hour of deepest need.

I know that if she were free today my mother would, in thanking you, also ask you to pray that the oppressors and the oppressed should throw down their weapons and join together to build a nation founded on humanity in the spirit of peace.

Although my mother is often described as a political dissident who strives by peaceful means for democratic change, we should remember that her quest is basically spiritual. As she has said, "The quintessential revolution is that of the spirit," and she has written of the "essential spiritual aims" of the struggle. The realisation of this depends solely on human responsibility. At the root of that responsibility lies, and I quote, "the concept of perfection, the urge to achieve it, the intelligence to find a path towards it, and the will to follow that path if not to the end, at least the distance needed to rise above individual limitation. . . ." "To live the full life," she says, "one must have the courage to bear the responsibility of the needs of others . . . one must want to bear this responsibility." And she links this firmly to her faith when she writes, ". . . Buddhism, the foundation of traditional Burmese culture, places the greatest value on man, who alone of all beings can achieve the supreme state of Buddhahood. Each man has in him the potential to realize the truth through his own will and endeavour and to help others to realize it." Finally she says, "The quest for democracy in Burma is the struggle of a people to live whole, meaningful lives as free and equal members of the world community. It is part of the unceasing human endeavour to prove that the spirit of man can transcend the flaws of his nature."

This is the second time that my younger brother and I have accepted a great prize for my mother in Norway. Last year we travelled to Bergen to receive for her the Thorolf Rafto Prize for Human Rights, a wonderful prelude to this year's event. By now we have a very special feeling for the people of Norway. It is my hope that soon my mother will be able to share this feeling and to speak directly for herself instead of through me. Meanwhile this tremendous support for her and the people of Burma has served to bring together two peoples from opposite ends of the earth. I believe much will follow from the links now forged.

It only remains for me to thank you all from the bottom of my heart. Let us hope and pray that from today the wounds start to heal and that in the years to come the 1991 Nobel Prize for Peace will be seen as a historic step towards the achievement of true peace in Burma. The lessons of the past will not be forgotten, but it is our hope for the future that we celebrate today.

Source: Aung San Suu Kyi, Acceptance Speech. Available at http://
nobelprize.org/nobel_prizes/peace/laureates/1991/kyi-acceptance
.html. © 1991 The Nobel Foundation.

1942	**September 6** Aung San and Ma Khin Kyi marry.
1945	**June 19** Aung San Suu Kyi is born.
1947	**July 19** General Aung San is gunned down, along with several other cabinet members.
1948	**January 4** Burma earns independence and is officially named the Independent Union of Burma.
1952	Aung San Lin, Suu's brother, accidently drowns.
1953	Ma Khin Kyi is appointed Burma's first minister of social welfare.
1960	Ma Khin Kyi is appointed ambassador to India; the family moves to New Delhi.
1962	Suu Kyi attends Delhi University, where she studies politics; General Ne Win seizes control of Burma in a military coup.
1964	Ne Win eliminates all political parties and establishes the Burma Socialist Program Party (BSPP); Suu Kyi moves to Great Britain and begins her studies at St. Hugh's College, Oxford University; while in England, Suu Kyi meets Michael Aris.
1967	Suu Kyi earns her bachelor of arts degree in philosophy, politics, and economics.
1969–1971	Suu Kyi moves to New York City to continue graduate studies, but instead gets a job as Assistant Secretary, Advisory Committee on Administrative and Budgetary Questions, United Nations Secretariat.

1972	**January 1** Suu Kyi marries Michael Aris; the couple moves to Bhutan; Suu Kyi takes a job as research officer in the Royal Ministry of Foreign Affairs.
1973	Suu Kyi and her husband return to England, where she gives birth to their first child, son Alexander.
1974	Michael accepts a research appointment in Tibetan and Himalayan studies at Oxford University.
1977	Suu Kyi gives birth to the couple's second son, Kim; during this time, she begins to research her father's life to write a biography about him.
1984	University of Queensland Press publishes Suu Kyi's book, *Aung San,* in *Leaders of Asia* series.
1985–1986	Suu Kyi travels to Japan, where she works as a visiting scholar at Kyoto University's Center for Southeast Asian Studies; son Kim goes with her, while son Alexander goes to India with Michael, who has received a fellowship at the Indian Institute of Advanced Studies.
1987	Suu Kyi is awarded a fellowship at the Indian Institute of Advanced Studies, where the family is reunited; family moves back to Oxford, and Suu Kyi enrolls at London School of Oriental and African Studies to work on advanced degree.
1988	**March 31** Suu Kyi learns of her mother's stroke by phone and flies to Rangoon to care for her mother in the hospital; when Ma Khin Kyi is released from the hospital in June, Suu Kyi moves into her home on University Avenue.

108

August 8 The military junta in Myanmar responds to a mass uprising by killing thousands of protesters.

August 15 Suu Kyi writes a letter to the Burmese government requesting multiparty elections.

September 18 In response, the military establishes the State Law and Order Restoration Council (SLORC).

September 24 With Suu Kyi's help, the National League for Democracy (NLD) is formed, with Suu Kyi as general secretary; she begins to give speeches to mass crowds throughout Burma despite government ban.

December 27 Ma Khin Kyi dies at age of 76.

1989   **July 20** Suu Kyi is placed under house arrest in Rangoon and is declared ineligible to hold elected office.

1990   **May 27** While Suu Kyi is still under house arrest, the NLD wins an open election; SLORC refuses to honor the results of the election and imprisons opposition party leaders.

1991   **December 10** Suu Kyi is awarded the Nobel Peace Prize while still in detention; Michael and sons Alexander and Kim accept the award on her behalf.

1995   **July 10** Suu Kyi is released from house arrest by the SLORC; she continues to speak out against the military dictatorship and calls for the election results to be upheld.

1999   Michael is diagnosed with cancer, but his request to visit his wife in Yangon is denied by the government; knowing she would be forbidden to return to Myanmar, Suu Kyi decides to stay in the country; Michael dies in London.

2000   Suu Kyi is again placed under house arrest after a standoff with police and the military while traveling outside Yangon.

        December 6 She is awarded the U.S. Presidential Medal of Freedom. Son Alexander accepts the award for his mother.

2002   **May 6** Suu Kyi is released from 18-month-long house arrest.

2003   **May 30** For the third time in 14 years, Suu Kyi is arrested.

2006   Although still under house arrest, Aung San Suu Kyi continues to speak out against the military government's policies; she is isolated by the regime from having contact with supporters within Myanmar and the international community, despite repeated calls for her release.

Chapter 1

1. "The Rise And Fall of Ne Win Dictatorship," KNU Bulletin No. 17, August 1988. Available online. URL: http://www.ibiblio.org/obl/docs3/KNUBulletin17.pdf.

2. Bettina Ling, *Aung San Suu Kyi: Standing Up for Democracy.* New York: The Feminist Press at The City University of New York, 1999, p. 53.

3. William Thomas, *Aung San Suu Kyi.* Milwaukee: World Almanac Library, 2005, p. 28.

4. Aung San Suu Kyi, *Freedom From Fear and Other Writings.* London: Viking/Penguin Group, 1991, p. 193.

Chapter 2

5. Asia Geographia. "An Introduction to Myanmar," Click and Explore: Myanmar. Available online. URL: http://www.geographia.com/myanmar/.

6. Rewata Dhamma, "Buddhism in Myanmar." Available online. URL: http://web.ukonline.co.uk/buddhism/rdhamma4.htm.

7. The Friends of the Western Buddhist Order. "What is Buddhism?" Available online. URL: http://www.fwbo.org/buddhism.html.

8. "What is a Pagoda?" Myanmars.net: Beliefs. Available online. URL: http://www.myanmars.net/belief/pagoda.htm.

Chapter 3

9. Encyclopedia Britannica Online. Myanmar: History: The British in Burma (1885–1948): "The Religious Dilemma," p. 37. Available online. URL: http://secure.britannica.com/eb/article-52605/Myanmar.

10. The Buddhist Channel. "Shoe Issue Which Paved the Way to the Independence Struggle in Burma." *Lanka Daily News,* December 25, 2004. Available online. URL: http://www.buddhistchannel.tv/index.php?id=8,482,0,0,1,0.

11. National Coalition Government of Union of Burma. "NLD Statement 170/1999: On the 79th anniversary of National Day," December 2, 1999. Available online. URL: http://www.ncgub.net/NLD_Statements/NLD%20Statement%20170,1999.htm.

12. Barbara Victor, *The Lady.* Boston: Faber and Faber, 1998, p. 60.

13. Aung San of Burma. "Perspectives: Life Sketch of the Author." Available online. URL: http://www.aungsan.com/SelfPortrait.htm.

14. Ibid.

Chapter 4

15. BBCBurmese.com. "The Blood-strewn Path: Burma's Early Journey to Independence. Episode 8. Available online. URL: http://www.bbc.co.uk/burmese/highlights/

story/2005/09/050829_
vjdayspecials.shtml.

16. Victor, *The Lady,* p. 70.

17. ENSCC Policy Paper. "The
New Panglong Initiative:
Rebuilding the Union of
Burma." Available online. URL:
http://www.ibiblio.org/obl/
docs/NewPanglongInitiative%5
B1%5D.htm.

18. Ling, *Standing Up for Democracy,* p. 29.

19. Whitney Stewart, *Aung San Suu
Kyi: Fearless Voice of Burma.*
Minneapolis: Lerner Publishing
Group, 1997, p. 29.

Chapter 5

20. Aung San Suu Kyi, *Freedom
From Fear and Other Writ-
ings.* London: Viking/Penguin
Group, 1991, p. 18.

21. Ibid., p. 247.

22. Wikipedia, the free encyclopedia. "Mahatma Gandhi."
Available online. URL:
http://en.wikipedia.org/wiki/
Mahatma_Gandhi.

23. Victor, *The Lady,* p. 76.

24. Suu Kyi, *Freedom From Fear,* p.
242.

Chapter 6

25. Ibid., p. 250.

26. Ibid., pp. 250–251.

27. Ibid., p. xvii.

28. Ibid., p. 264.

29. Htay Kywe, "March Revolution
in Burma–I." *Democratic Voice
of Burma.* Available online.

URL: http://english.dvb.no/
news.php?id=4249.

30. Ibid.

31. Ibid.

Chapter 7

32. Victor, *The Lady,* p. 4.

33. Ne Win, "The Extraordinary
Session of the BSPP Congress,
23–25 July 1988." "The Burma
Press Summary," Available
online. URL: http://www
.ibiblio.org/obl/docs/BSPP_
Congress.htm.

34. Victor, *The Lady,* pp. 83–84.

35. Alan Clements and Leslie Kean.
*Burma's Revolution of Spirit:
The Struggle for Democratic
Freedom and Dignity.* New
York: Aperture Foundation,
1994, p. 36.

36. Ibid., pp. 36, 42.

37. Ibid., p. 42.

38. Suu Kyi, *Freedom From Fear,* p.
xviii.

39. Victor, *The Lady,* p. 82.

40. Suu Kyi, *Freedom From Fear,* p.
193.

41. Ibid., p. 200.

42. Ibid., p. xviii.

Chapter 8

43. Clements and Kean, *The Struggle for Democratic Freedom and
Dignity,* p. 57.

44. Victor, *The Lady,* p. 94.

45. Ibid., p. 95.

46. Clements and Kean, *The Struggle for Democratic Freedom and
Dignity,* p. 50.

47. European Parliament. "Human Rights Unit: The Sakharov Prize for Freedom of Thought." Available online. URL: http://www.europarl.europa.eu/comparl/afet/droi/sakharov/default.htm.

48. Ling, *Standing Up for Democracy,* p. 76.

49. Alexander Aris, "Nobel Peace Prize Acceptance Speech." Available online. URL: http://nobelprize.org/nobel_prizes/peace/laureates/1991/kyi-acceptance.html.

Chapter 9

50. Barbara Bradley, "Dark Victory in Burma," *Vogue Magazine* (October 1995).

51. Peace Media Service. "Nobel Laureates Urge Release of Suu Kyi." *Nonviolent Sanctions, News From the Albert Einstein Institution,* Vol. IV, No. 3, Winter 1992/1993. Available online. URL: http://www.aeinstein.org/organizations/org/13_winter92_93-1.pdf.

52. Victor, *The Lady,* p. 132.

53. "Those Who Pushed to Free Aung San Suu Kyi." July 20, 1994. Available online. URL: http://www.ibiblio.org/freeburma/assk/assk3-4f.html.

54. Ibid.

55. Ibid.

56. Victor, *The Lady,* p. 138.

57. Thomas, *Aung San Suu Kyi,* p. 38.

58. The New Courier, "Aung San Suu Kyi: 'We've got to move forward,'" April 2003. Available online. URL: http://portal.unesco.org/es/ev.php-URL_ID=10384&URL_DO=DO_TOPIC&URL_SECTION=201.html.

59. Colin Powell, "It's Time to Turn the Tables on Burma's Thugs." U.S. Department of State, *The Wall Street Journal,* June 12, 2003. Available online. URL: http://www.state.gov/secretary/former/powell/remarks/2003/21466.htm.

60. "Daw Aung San Suu Kyi: An Icon, Inspiration and Unifier for Peace: A Tribute & Call for Freedom on her 60th Birthday," June 19, 2005. Available online. URL: http://www.aseanmp.org/resources/ASSK60bday.pdf.

BIBLIOGRAPHY

Clements, Alan and Leslie Kean. *Burma's Revolution of Spirit: The Struggle for Democratic Freedom and Dignity.* New York: Aperture Foundation, Inc., 1994.

Ling, Bettina. *Aung San Suu Kyi: Standing Up for Democracy.* New York: The Feminist Press at The City University of New York, 1999.

Stewart, Whitney. *Aung San Suu Kyi: Fearless Voice of Burma.* Minneapolis, Minn.: Lerner Publishing Group, 1997.

Suu Kyi, Aung San. *Freedom From Fear and Other Writings.* London: Viking/Penguin Group, 1991.

———. *Letters From Burma.* New York: Penguin Books, 1997.

Suu Kyi, Aung San, and Alan Clement. *The Voice of Hope.* New York: Seven Stories Press, 1998.

Thomas, William. *Aung San Suu Kyi.* Milwaukee, Wisc: World Almanac Library, 2005.

Victor, Barbara. *The Lady.* Boston: Faber and Faber, 1998.

Books

Alldritt, Leslie D. *Buddhism.* Philadelphia: Chelsea House, 2004.

Keane, Ann T. *Peacemakers: Winners of the Nobel Peace Prize.* New York: Oxford University Press, 1998.

Severence, John. *Gandhi, Great Soul.* New York: Clarion Books, 1997.

Stewart, Whitney. *Aung San Suu Kyi: Fearless Voice of Burma.* Minneapolis, Minn.: Lerner Publishing Group, 1997.

Suu Kyi, Aung San. *Letters From Burma.* New York: Penguin Books, 1997.

Suu Kyi, Aung San, and Alan Clement. *The Voice of Hope.* New York: Seven Stories Press, 1998.

Wright, David. *Burma.* Danbury, Conn.: Children's Press, 1991.

Yin, Saw Myat. *Myanmar.* New York: Benchmark Books, 2001.

Web Sites

Aung San
http://www.aungsan.com/

Aung San Suu Kyi Web site
http://www.dassk.com/

Buddhist Information and Education Network
http://www.buddhanet.net/

CIA World Factbook—Burma
http://worldebookfair.com/Members/Government_Library/CIA_Reading_
Room/2002factbook/print/bm.html

An Introduction to Myanmar
http://www.geographia.com/myanmar/

The Nobel Peace Prize Web site
http://nobelpeaceprize.org/

TimeAsia: Asian Heroes—Aung San Suu Kyi
http://www.time.com/time/asia/features/heroes/suukyi.html

The United Nations
http://www.un.org/english/

PICTURE CREDITS

INDEX

JUDY L. HASDAY, a native of Philadelphia, received her B.A. in communications and her Ed.M. in instructional technologies from Temple University. Ms. Hasday has written dozens of books for young adults, including the New York Public Library "Books for the Teen Age" award winners *James Earl Jones* (1999) and *The Holocaust* (2003), and the National Social Studies Council "2001 Notable Social Studies Trade Book for Young People" award winner, *Extraordinary Women Athletes.* Her free time is devoted to photography, travel, and her pets: her cat, Sassy, and four zebra finches, Scotch, B.J., Atticus, and Jacob.